# Beyond Tears

# Beyond Tears

## Living After Losing a Child

**Revised Edition**

Carol Barkin

Audrey Cohen

Lorenza Colletti

Barbara Eisenberg

Barbara J. Goldstein

Madelaine (Maddy) Perri Kasden

Phyllis Levine

Ariella Long

Rita Volpe

**As told to Ellen Mitchell**

 St. Martin's Griffin ❦ New York

BEYOND TEARS, REVISED EDITION. Copyright © 2004, 2009 by Ellen Mitchel, Carol Barkin, et al. All rights reserved. Printed in the United States of America. For information, address St. Martin's Press, 175 Fifth Avenue, New York, N.Y. 10010.

www.stmartins.com

Library of Congress Cataloging-in-Publication Data

Beyond tears : living after losing a child / Carol Barkin . . . [et al.] ; as told to Ellen Mitchell.—Rev. ed.
    p. cm.
  ISBN-13: 978-0-312-54519-2
  ISBN-10: 0-312-54519-3
  1. Bereavement—Psychological aspects. 2. Children—Death—Psychological aspects. 3. Mothers—Psychology. I. Barkin, Carol, 1943– II. Mitchell, Ellen, 1938–
    BF575.G7B482   2009
    155.9'37—dc22

                              2008049931

20   19   18   17   16   15   14

# In Memoriam

**JESSICA COHEN**  1979–1995
*(daughter of Audrey and Irwin Cohen)*

**MARC COLLETTI**  1968–1995
*(son of Lorenza and Joseph Colletti)*

**BRIAN EISENBERG**  1974–1996
*(son of Barbara and Michael Eisenberg)*

**HOWARD GOLDSTEIN**  1970–1991
*(son of Barbara and Bruce Goldstein)*

**LISA BARKIN GOOTMAN**  1967–1995
*(daughter of Carol and Donald Barkin)*

**ANDREA LEVINE**  1965–1987
*(daughter of Phyllis and Melvin Levine)*

**MICHAEL LONG**  1975–1995
*(son of Ariella and Robert Long)*

**NEILL PERRI**  1971–1995
*(son of Madelaine Perri Kasden and John Perri,
stepson of Clifford Kasden and Mary Speed Perri)*

**MICHAEL VOLPE**  1967–1987
*(son of Rita and Thomas Volpe)*

# Contents

# Acknowledgments

We are ever grateful to that intimate circle of family and friends who surrounded us and supported us in our early grief and have stayed on. As the years pass by and others tend to forget, these special few are always there to share a memory, a tear or a laugh.

We thank our agent, Bob Markel, a truly gentle man. His inner fortitude is made all the stronger by his keen understanding of the vicissitudes of life. Who but Bob could have remained unruffled and in good humor in the face of nine bereaved mothers and their collaborator, all of us anxious, first-time authors? He provided unflagging confidence even as we were unsure of ourselves.

We acknowledge those who walked us through the process at St. Martin's Press. Editor Jennifer Weis saw instinctively that this book is more than just a paean to our lost children, that it carries a vital message for the too many others who must bear such a tragedy. Assistant editor Stefanie Lindskog has offered sage advice and answered questions that only neophyte authors could ask. We thank her for her unfailing patience and constant good cheer.

We are indebted to the Compassionate Friends organization. We nine first met there and later went on to form our own bond. The Compassionate Friends group is a major factor in the healing process for thousands of bereaved parents throughout the nation. Information about Compassionate Friends can be found at 877-969-0010 or on the Web at www.compassionatefriends.org.

To our husbands, whose input is an integral part of this book. We thank them for their unconditional love and understanding.

To our surviving children, who have had to endure far more than young people should ever have to endure. There were times when you had to become the parent to us and help us along the way. We love you more than mere words can express.

We are grateful to each other. The nine of us are each other's support network. We have leaned on one another from the early days of our bereavement; we will likely lean on one another throughout the rest of our lives. We are each other's alter egos and each other's best friends.

There were times when one or more of us found that calling up painful details for this book was just too much to bear and would gladly have given up the project. But we kept at it, thanks much to the gentle prodding of Phyllis Levine, our catalyst. In turn, each of us thanks the other for their unique and valuable contributions to these pages. Without one and all, there would be no book.

We thank our lost children for smiling down on us. We can hear them saying, "Way to go, Ma."

# Mothers of the Mourning After

When we met we could barely speak, paralyzed and frozen we sat.

We leaned on one another and were able to stand,

And slowly we learned to walk.

As time passed a bond formed from the love of our children lost,

A friendship forged in pain grew into love and laughter.

Together we have found new ways to live and love and remember the life.

Longing for a time that exists in heart's memory, together we talk of our children
    and smile with silent tears.

Dear friend, thank you for walking the valley with me.

Thank you for sharing the love.

As we climb together we can see ahead more clearly.

We can see them in the distance smiling, waiting and proud.

If we could only touch them. . . . until then we hold . . . one another.

*Rita Volpe*

# Beyond Tears

# Introduction

There are certain truisms in life. One of them is that it goes against the natural order of things to bury one's child. However, as bereaved mothers we can no longer believe in natural order. Our comfortable, secure lives, our innocence, all were shattered with the deaths of our children. Now our reality is upside down, inside out and far removed from what we thought it would be.

Each day is a learning experience in a course we never signed up for, in a life we never anticipated. Along the way, we have each acquired some degree of healing, and we have reached a point in the road where we can now share what we have endured. We hope our stories will shed some light for others who find themselves walking the same dark path.

This, then, is a book that no one ever envisions needing. It talks of how we wake each day and pass the hours when there seems scant reason to do so. It tells of how we go on when going on appears pointless, and it explores ways in which we manage to exist when our lives seem hollow and we are left to wonder . . . why me? Why my child?

We are nine women of similar backgrounds; we all lost children who were teens or young adults. They died as the result of either illness or accident. Although we had never met before our sons and daughters were taken from us, we eventually gravitated to one another as we searched desperately for understanding.

Now we are a large part of each other's lives. We meet regularly for dinner. We endure mutual pain. We phone each other at all times of day and night. We sit together for hours—listening, writing, reading and listening some more. As a group, we revisit places that others have long forgotten, but which we cannot bear to leave behind.

We have survived in concert with one another, even when we were in such deep despair that we wondered if our lives were worth living and contemplated suicide. We leaned on one another when we could barely place one foot in front of the other if we had tried to stand alone. We owe our inner grit and spirit to the fact that we have shared our ordeal and bonded together.

We have discovered the sad truth that beyond our own circle there is very little realistic and substantive help for those who grieve for the loss of a child. We have each found a crushing lack of awareness and understanding among many whom we should have been able to depend upon such as medical personnel, clergy, social workers, bereavement counselors and in some cases even family and friends.

In this book, we share the practical approaches we take when people fail to be of help. We tell how we have learned to get through holidays and what used to be joyous family occasions. We discuss the changes that have occurred in our relationships with our spouses, our other children and the entire family dynamic.

We also voice our opinions of those who take their cue from the pop culture of our times to tell us it is time for us to "get on with our lives" and find "closure." Indeed, since the horrors of 9/11, "closure" seems to have become the watchword of therapists, politicians, journalists and television analysts alike. These "civilians," our name for those who have not experienced the death of a child, have no idea what they are speaking about when they use this term. We the experts know all too well that there is no such thing as "closure" following the senseless and untimely death of a child.

We have much to share. We know the value of a day's work in order to keep our thoughts from becoming mired down in our personal tragedies. We have learned how to react when a stranger asks, "How many children do you have?" We share what we do when a longtime acquaintance crosses the street to avoid the uneasiness of having to chat with us.

We know how hard it is to face our dead child's bedroom and his or her favorite breakfast cereal. We deal with demons that come in the night and clumsy neighbors who come in the day. We memorialize our children by wearing their jewelry and by setting up foundations in their names.

Because it is our hope that this book will be read by grieving couples and their family members, as well as counselors, clerics and others, we have included the views voiced by the fathers of our children. Much as we women have been there for each other through the years so, too, our husbands have become well acquainted and supportive of one another. In some ways, their manner of experiencing and expressing grief parallels our own, but in other respects is in marked contrast to our own.

While our stories are different in detail, they are similar in sum. Many of you probably have stories and needs much like ours. We know we can be a source of comfort to you. We have found there is much to be gained in just realizing there are others who have experienced the same horror and felt, as we all did, that they would not be able to keep a grip on their sanity.

There is no clear road map for passing through parental bereavement. However, there is a path that takes us from relentless grief to what we now call "shadow grief." "Shadow grief" is always with us, but it is bearable. We are helping each other along that path.

It is our love for our lost children that has given us the inspiration, the strength and the determination to put our thoughts and our words into book form. We have to believe our children made a difference in their far too short lives on this earth. They are with us every step of the way, and it is their memory and guidance that has helped us to develop this book, in which we share with you some of what has helped us to get beyond our tears.

## JESSICA RACHEL COHEN

Jessie was my only child, not that that makes her story any more or less important than the others—that's just the way it was.

Funny, but I always thought of her birth date, 7/11, as my lucky number, and I guess it was . . . just to have had her for those years. It's the only way I can think. After she died, we learned that a great many others whose lives she touched in her short life felt just as we did.

As far back as nursery school, Jessie knew who she was and where she wanted to be. She was never bored; life was her playground. She was content to be by herself, and she was just as content hanging out with her friends. She was interested in everything and loved learning. At parent-teacher conferences she made me proud. I loved being Jessica's mom.

Jessie's faith in nature was boundless. At the age of four, she asked my husband, Irwin (we call him Irv) if she could plant a kernel of popcorn. He explained that the kernel was overprocessed and could not possibly grow. Not to be thwarted, she dug a small hole and planted a single kernel smack in the middle of our backyard. Irv spent the rest of the summer mowing around the corn that sprang up in the midst of our lawn.

Jessie could pop the seedpods of impatiens plants or make an impression of a leaf using sunlight on photo-sensitive paper. She planted watermelons, cantaloupes and splashes of colorful flowers, among them the bleeding hearts that still bloom and tug at our heartstrings every spring. All these years later we continue to reap the fruits of Jessie's garden.

In high school, Jess oversaw her school's video production program. She was always behind the camera, according to her television production teacher, who described Jessie as "one of the greatest kids I have ever known." Today there is an annual video production award given to a deserving student because of a memorializing fund set up by that teacher.

I know I am a doting mom, and I don't want to leave the impression that Jessie was perfect . . . far from it. But she was a very special treasure.

Jess was poised and confident. She had a beautiful, though untrained, singing voice. She played the guitar, she played softball, she was a member of Mathletes, her school's competitive math team, and from the fifth grade forward, when she first came to know the story of our country's founding, she dreamed of becoming an American history teacher.

She was patient and kind, and possessed strong convictions and a beautiful sense of decency. She was a true friend but fiercely independent. Who but a teenager with a quirky sense of humor would teach their dog Clyde to communicate? She would surreptitiously tickle his neck so that he appeared to be shaking his head no in response to questions, usually of the "do you like so and so?" variety.

It all ended on June 30, 1995, when Jessie was eleven days shy of her sixteenth birthday.

We were visiting my husband's sister and her husband in the Poconos. We had driven up the night before and stopped at my stepdaughter's home. Irv had just taken retirement from Grumman, and Jess had just finished her sophomore year. A friend of hers, Krishma, was along with us.

It's odd the things you remember afterward. I remember Krishma and Jessie sitting in the backseat of the car talking, and Jessie asking Krishma, who is of the Sikh faith, how anyone could agree to an arranged marriage. Krishma told her you just accepted what your life was supposed to be. I don't know why I remember that.

We were up early that morning. It was so peaceful. We watched a family of deer grazing in the woods behind the house. Jessie was feeling good and she made breakfast for everyone. Our conversation turned to what we wanted to do that day. Someone suggested golf, someone else said shopping. Jessie wanted to water-ski. My brother-in-law had a small boat and a pair of water skis that Jess had tried a couple of times before. I think she had stood up on them for a split second once, but she was never able to stay up. We decided to take her waterskiing early, before the July 4 weekend crowds arrived.

My sister-in-law and I stayed onshore because my brother-in-law thought too many people in the boat would make it harder for Jessie to get up on the skis. We played Scrabble, and in the distance I could see Jessie and Krishma swimming near the boat. Then I didn't see them anymore. The lake was still and almost deserted.

At one point, I did see someone water-skiing and I jumped up and asked, "Is that Jessie?" My sister-in-law said, "You're always so nervous." But I just didn't feel right. I was jittery, maybe because I was never comfortable in the water. Not like Jess. She was a good swimmer. She had no problem with the water.

We had been there an hour or so when the boat pulled up and my brother-in-law was yelling, "She went down, she was hit. Call 911, get an ambulance!" I thought he was kidding, then I realized he wasn't. I didn't know what to do first. Should I run to the boathouse? Should I go to Irv? I pounded on my brother-in-law's chest because he didn't want me to go to Jessie. But I ran to her anyway and she was just lying there in the boat. I started screaming, "Please, Jessie, please, don't die." Irv, who had dove in and pulled Jess out of the water, was telling me there was no pulse, no breathing . . . nothing.

Jessie died when she was struck by a jet ski propelled by a mentally and physically challenged young woman who was left unsupervised. Her father later said he was sure he had locked the watercraft securely. But we don't believe that. We never had a personal word from that young woman's family, no letter, no apology. I can't forgive that.

Maybe if someone else had been driving the boat. Maybe if I'd been out there. Maybe I could have seen something, done something. You turn the story over and over in your mind.

After Jessie's death, at her high school memorial service, her English literature teacher said of Jessica, "Because she was in my life, I am a better teacher, a better mother, a better friend, a better person. She will unquestionably live forever."

Would that she had.

Audrey Cohen

*One*

# The Mourning After:
# The First Year

We were studies in contrast in those early months. We were filled with rage and yet we felt hollow. Our eyes brimmed with tears and yet they were empty. We could scream but speech came rarely, if at all. We were in excruciating pain and yet we were numb. Our self-esteem was beaten down and our trust shattered, but there was no one who could console us. There was no place to feel secure. We tried to crawl inside ourselves, but even that afforded us no place to hide. It was as if our very being died along with that of our children. We were and remain forever changed.

*Carol: "I had an earlier photo of myself on my driver's license. I looked at the eyes. I was a different person before Lisa died."*

Whatever we did during that first year was done from behind a veil of shock. Indeed, if we had to pick one word, one emotion that imbued our minds, our thoughts, our very being in that horrible first year, it would be shock. In some ways it obviously insulated us because we learned later that what we thought was the worst possible pain could from time to time become even more acute as our lives unfolded.

If there was any sensation at all that permeated the cocoon of shock in which we wrapped ourselves it was exhaustion. Our bodies were encased in a relentless fatigue that left us drained of energy and debilitated during the days, but refused to allow us the luxury of restorative sleep at night.

In that first year, we all refused to accept the finality of the death of our children, and some of us never will. It seemed that our existence had become surreal; it was as if we were each having an out-of-body experience. We wanted to wake up and find it was not true. . . . This could not be our life.

*Phyllis: "In that first year, I couldn't bring myself to say 'killed.' I talked about loss. Only later could I say that Andrea was alone in the car and she was killed by an eighteen-year-old who didn't know what he was doing. Only fifteen years later did I request a copy of the medical examiner's report."*

We speak of the "first year" but actually attempting to define a first year is disingenuous. There is no universal calendar by which to gauge grief. With the passage of time, we have learned that the reactions of the bereaved differ from person to person depending on where they are in their grief. Medical personnel, clergy, counselors well-meaning but misguided acquaintances may tell you that you can expect to feel better by such-and-such a date, but they are wrong. No such timeline exists.

*Barbara G.: "There is no schedule for when you'll start to feel better. It's as if a scab forms over a wound; it can be reopened by the slightest trigger."*

*Barbara E.: "It took me five years to even talk to my colleagues at work about it. Five years seemed to be some kind of a milestone for me."*

*Maddy: "You have reached a new level when your first thought is of your child's life rather than a replay of their death."*

Early on you will have to fortify yourself against insensitive comments from blundering friends, relatives and acquaintances, some of whom should know better and others who have no idea that you are bereaved. Even seemingly benign questions such as "how are you?" or "how was your summer?," or comments such as "have a good day," will stab into you and throw you off balance.

There is a cold chill that goes through your body each time some unthinking acquaintance tells you "it's time to get over it." There is no "getting over it." You will carry every detail of what happened throughout every day of your life, and you will forevermore categorize all events as occurring either "before" or "after" your child's death. The memory of your son or daughter is all that remains of them here on earth, and certainly if they were still alive you would think of them each day and worry about their well-being.

*Audrey: "In fact, when your children are here you tend to take them for granted. When they are gone you think of them twenty-four hours a day."*

*Ariella: "You almost expect your child to call you and awaken you from the nightmare."*

Each of us has had to find our own way to accept the reality of our child's death. The best hope is that you will be able to hold close the beautiful recollections and let go of some of the dreadfulness.

In the first months, the pain is raw and there is no escaping it. There are a couple of unlikely places, however, where we all were able to achieve some small measure of release. Surprisingly, we took to the car and to the shower for refuge. Both were hideaways where we could scream out loud.

*Rita: "In my car, I screamed at the top of my lungs with hair-raising shrieks. At the end of the school day, I looked forward to that moment. People would look at me and think I was singing to my car radio."*

*Lorenza: "It was like an explosion, that moment, that privacy."*

*Phyllis: "My tears made me drive blind."*

*Ariella: "I screamed in agony in the shower and in the car. I couldn't comprehend that Michael was really gone. I kept crying out, 'This can't be happening.'"*

*Barbara G.: "I felt free to stand in the shower and say whatever I wanted. The water would drown me out."*

Some of us drove recklessly. We raced red lights. We felt no fear;

why should we—we had already experienced the worst that could happen. We drove as if on autopilot, not cognizant of where we were going or how we got there. We were never fully aware of the moment. As we drove, our minds raced to thoughts of our children and our pain. Sometimes our imaginations took over completely, and we thought we saw our children driving by. We saw them everywhere, but found them nowhere.

*Ariella: "I remember sitting in the car and seeing someone who looked exactly like Michael, his hair, his hand movements. I didn't want the light to change. I just kept staring at him. In my head it was Michael. I followed him for a while thinking if I could just stop him and convince him to go to a diner and talk to me I would have some connection to Michael. And then I thought to myself, 'You're crazy. Let it go.' "*

Searching for our children, or for some indication of their existence, consumed much of our time in those early days and months. We heard their voices in our heads. We wanted to be able to reach out and touch them. We ached to feel their physical presence.

*Lorenza: "I needed to hear Marc say Ma just the way he always did. I'd go to sleep at night hearing him say that."*

*Rita: "I needed to touch my son. It was a universal feeling. We all constantly looked for our children, as if they were misplaced somewhere."*

*Audrey: "We looked for signs. If a light flickered, it meant Jess was there. She was always there. She followed me."*

*Ariella: "We all still believe they exist. I have to have a place where my child is. They don't cease to exist. We need to know our kids are okay."*

*Maddy: "One evening, my husband and I saw a young man who resembled Neill. He sat like Neill. He moved like Neill. I couldn't take my eyes off him."*

We sought help in places we would never even have considered in our previous lives.

*Lorenza: "I had never heard of a psychic before. But in the first year we all went to psychics."*

*Audrey: "I think there is always the hope that the psychic will connect you to your child."*

*Ariella: "I didn't focus on what the psychic got wrong. I focused on what she*

*got right. And some of it was quite amazing. I was able to cry, and had a feeling
I was really talking to Michael. It was cathartic, like a telephone call."*

Rita: *"Whether it was true or not, it helped."*

Laughter was gone from our world. Now, years later, we laugh . . .
mostly when we are with each other. The fact that we are able to laugh
at all can oftentimes shock "the civilian world"—those who are not bereaved parents.

Listening to music was unbearable.

*Lorenza: "In the car I would listen to talk radio. Talk radio saved me. To this
day, at home I fall asleep with my talk radio. Never any music."*

*Maddy: "Music became an emotional trigger. In that first year, most love
songs and songs about breakups and broken hearts seemed to fit our lives and the
loss of our children, and they still do."*

*Ariella: "The words will get you and cut you to pieces. You'll hear your
child's favorite song, or the words take you to a place that is just too painful. You
don't want the joy of music. You deny yourself."*

Euphemisms that we once took with a grain of salt became watch-
words during those early months. We'd all heard the expression "your
skin crawls"; ours did. We'd all used the phrase "with a heavy heart" or
"a hole in the heart." These things became all too true.

*Rita: "I could not deal with the fact that my son was under the ground. It
made my skin crawl."*

*Audrey: "My body would crawl. I'd pull off my clothes, my shoes."*

*Lorenza: "The heavy heart was like a heavy coat. It was always there. It
never lifted."*

The pain we felt was actual physical pain, made all the worse by the
mental anguish and oppressive and constant exhaustion. We were subject to panic attacks, headaches, bouts of piercing stomach pain and
changed eating habits.

*Carol: "I had difficulty breathing. I was constantly sighing out loud. There's
no refuge from the pain. You crave peace and there is none. It's an awful place to
be. The pain is unrelenting."*

*Phyllis: "I was so exhausted; it was an effort to live."*

*Barbara E.: "For the first few months, my husband and I didn't leave the house. It was difficult to even sit up. We spent our days and nights sleeping on the family room couches. When I returned to work after three months, I didn't have the energy or concentration to finish the day. At lunchtime, I would race home and collapse on the sofa. After sleeping awhile, I would return to work and count the minutes until I could return to the sofa."*

*Audrey: "I forced myself to go to work. Then I would leave abruptly in midday and go home. I would read and fall asleep on the sofa. Then I'd wake up and go back to work, forcing myself to finish out the day."*

*Rita: "I'd fall asleep and wake up with a jolt. I'd wake up five or six times, and each time it kept coming back to me as a brand-new shock. It would always be new."*

*Barbara G.: "One of the things that made me so tired was just going through the motions of living out the day. I felt so tired. But the nights were even worse."*

*Audrey: "I'd lie there and relive what happened . . . like a tape in my mind."*

*Barbara G.: "The tape would play over and over. We were always waiting for a different ending."*

*Lorenza: "It was like wearing a heavy mask all day, knowing I had to pretend. I think just carrying around that mask made me tired."*

*Rita: "I'd have panic attacks at the supermarket whenever something triggered a thought of Michael when I wasn't expecting it. We all thought we were going crazy. We were bombarded with feelings we couldn't even name. We couldn't get our right foot in front of our left."*

*Barbara G.: "It was difficult to swallow food and I lost much too much weight. It seemed as though my muscles had collapsed. My acute vision suffered. The shock to the physical body is very real. I was told that whenever I see a new doctor, I should tell him or her that I am a bereaved mother. It is a part of my medical history."*

Indeed, the ground beneath our feet took on new meaning, especially the hallowed ground in which we had just buried our children. Some of us were obsessed with going to the cemetery, others were obsessed with staying away. One of us still has not been able to visit her child's grave. Snow and rain falling on our children's graves was almost too much to bear.

*Barbara G.:* "*Oh God, the first time it rained, Bruce had to pull me into the house. I said, 'I can't be here. I have to go and hold an umbrella over Howie. It's raining outside and my son is in the ground.' "*

*Phyllis:* "*I couldn't walk on the grass for that same reason.*"

*Lorenza:* "*When there was no stone at the cemetery, I could almost deal with it, but when the stone was put up and his name was engraved there, then it was written in stone.*"

*Phyllis:* "*I had just the opposite reaction. When Andrea's gravestone was set in place, I felt as though I was visiting her there at her place.*"

*Barbara E.:* "*Cemeteries close to the public at night. We broke in. One night our need was so great that my husband climbed a ten-foot fence to water the flowers on Brian's gravesite.*"

*Ariella:* "*I have never been to the cemetery. I do not believe Michael is there. I believe his soul is free and his body is not there. If I really thought Michael was there, I could not live.*"

The seasons changed and we resented it. Our surroundings and our lives, which had always existed in living color, became drab and gray.

*Carol:* "*I didn't care about anything. All the things that once seemed so important were no longer important.*"

We neglected ourselves, we wore no makeup and lost all concern for personal appearance. We refused to pose for photographs. We wore the same clothing day after day. The only clothing that mattered to us was that of our dead children. We could not bring ourselves to clean the dirty laundry we found in their bedrooms. We needed to keep some vestige of their smells, their looks, their existence.

*Barbara E.:* "*I slept with the pillow Brian died on for a short while and then put it on the chair in my bedroom. I was afraid to get it dirty and have to wash away his smell.*"

*Rita:* "*I could not wash Michael's smell out of my life. I hugged his bed, his clothes. I kept his worn clothes in the hamper and refused to empty it.*"

*Maddy:* "*I have the pajamas Neill slept in the night before he died.*"

*Barbara G.: "I never wear happy colors . . . no reds, no yellows, no more. How did the sun come up the next day?"*

*Lorenza: "How dare the tulips grow?"*

*Ariella: "Spring hurt that first year and it still hurts, but not as much. Now I love the winter when it's rainy and dreary."*

While we ignored most of our surroundings in that first year, we became obsessive about certain routines. Of course, family rituals we had cherished in the past that marked birthdays, anniversaries and holidays were completely torn apart and discarded. In that first year, we could not bring ourselves to even think about celebrating anything. Eventually, we found new and extremely different ways to commemorate special days, holidays and family occasions. Meanwhile, we obsessed over daily routines as a way of getting through each day.

*Rita: "We ate too much. We ate too little. We spent hours trying to get order back in our lives."*

*Phyllis: "We obsessed about everything. I obsessed about photographs. I told the cleaning lady not to touch any one of them."*

*Rita: "I went crazy looking everywhere for pictures of Michael."*

*Barbara G.: "I went around cleaning and then cleaning again. I think it was an attempt to bring some degree of control to my environment. I couldn't control what happened to my child, but I could control my surroundings."*

A number of us felt hostility to people who grew old. It is embarrassing to admit that one of us was actually embittered that her own parents were alive and well and in their eighties. We all experienced anguish about people who we felt were less deserving of life than our children.

*Rita: "When somebody elderly died, we not only didn't care about them, we resented them. They had so much more time than my son had."*

*Ariella: "I saw an old couple walking to the movies. My twenty-year-old son should have been able to go the movies."*

We grew resentful not only of the seasons, the elderly and the colors of the rainbow, but also of our religious beliefs. We are Jews and Christians, and each of us has questioned our God and asked why we have been punished in this way. In the first year, we turned to our religious leaders and, unfortunately, a number of us found them lacking in insight, with little to offer in the way of solace. While some of us were comforted by a positive response from our religious leaders, more of us were not. We asked our clerics if they had lost a child, feeling that unless they had experienced such a loss themselves, they could not fully understand the depths of our grief.

*Lorenza: "I wrote a letter to my priest and he sent me a poinsettia plant in response."*

*Barbara G.: "My rabbi asked me to come back to my Torah study group. I had always been spiritual and religious, and I really believed that if I was a good person a higher being would take care of my family. I kept my end of the bargain, but that higher being did not. When the rabbi asked me to come back, he said they missed me. Missed me? None of them even called up to see if I was alive or dead. They did meet Bruce in the supermarket one day and asked if we go out to dinner or anything. He said, 'Yes, we still eat.' They said they'd give us a call; they never did."*

*Maddy: "When Neill was alive, I always believed you don't pray to ask for things, you pray to give thanks. After Neill died, I thought I should have said, 'Don't kill my child.' That's when my anger really began and I never lost it."*

*Rita: "We all thought we did something wrong."*

*Audrey: "We searched our souls. Could we have been so evil that our children were punished for what we did."*

*Barbara G.: "When you were a child, your mother always told you that bad things would happen if you were bad. Why were our children punished instead of us?"*

*Rita: "I did have one priest tell me two words that helped. He said Michael 'is fine.' That helped me. And the principal of the school where I worked was a nun. She was so kind. She always remembered the anniversary of Michael's death. Eventually, she started a bereavement group at the school, and I know she did that because of me."*

*Barbara E.: "The rabbi from my temple, who'd known Brian from the time he was a little boy, came to our home to comfort us. He continued to phone us on a weekly basis. The temple started a bereavement group after that."*

At the time of our children's deaths, some of us lost respect for the hospital personnel with whom we came in contact. Sadly, that was sometimes true during our children's terminal illnesses, and also in emergency rooms following their accidental deaths. It is our fervent hope that people whose job is to deal with those experiencing tragedy will learn to grasp the depth of what bereaved parents are feeling at that terrible time and act accordingly.

*Maddy: "When we arrived at the hospital in New Jersey where they had taken Neill, we were told, 'The morgue is closed for the night. Come back in the morning.' Of course, we refused to take that for an answer, and eventually they did take us down to the morgue."*

*Audrey: "I insisted on riding in the ambulance, up front with the driver. Then the ambulance driver got lost on the way to the hospital. He kept telling me, 'Calm down, Mrs. Cohen.' How could I calm down with my daughter dying in the back of the ambulance?"*

*Lorenza: "I had to take my father to the hospital on the very day of my son's funeral. I spoke to the social worker at the hospital and told her of my grief. I was totally unable to function; I was distraught and needed help. She wasn't even listening to me. She was on the phone. She told me she'd be back in a few minutes. That was the social worker."*

*Barbara E.: "It seemed like everyone disappeared when my son died. We were left on our own to make contacts about where to turn for help. The hospital gave us no information."*

*Ariella: "The nurses and doctors turned their backs on us just before Michael died. No one came to assist us."*

*Carol: "Lisa's doctors couldn't or wouldn't acknowledge me in the hospital elevator."*

On the other hand, some of us found hospital personnel to be helpful.

*Phyllis: "The social worker who met us at the hospital was kind."*

*Barbara G.: "The hospital where Howie was dying was in Virginia. A nurse came and gave me information. She brought me soup. She said, 'You have to sleep and you have to eat. . . . You're going to have decisions to make.' She meant decisions about life support, organ transplants and an autopsy. Questions were all thrown at me within minutes of one another."*

In that first year, we learned that many of our social and professional relationships would change drastically, and not necessarily for the better. Of course, the opposite was also true, and sometimes comfort and genuinely warm friendship and understanding came from quarters where we least expected it.

*Barbara G.: "None of us would have known any of this if we were still in the civilian world. I have a friend who lost a child thirty-four years ago. I was her friend then, but I didn't know what to say to her. She had to phone all her friends and tell them that what she had wasn't catching, and that they could still come and visit her. She was one of the first people to appear at my door when my son was killed."*

*Lorenza: "I would teach one class, and then run into the corner and cry and let it all out. Some of the teachers would stop by and comfort me. I owe them a lot. Then I would go and teach the next class."*

*Barbara G.: "A colleague of mine would come to me at the end of each day and say, 'Put lipstick on, you're going home to your family. They worry about you.'"*

Most people who have not experienced a devastating loss mistakenly believe they should try to distract the newly bereaved and avoid talking about their grief. For the most part, we found that the world outside—the civilian world of intact families who have never lost a child—can be a terribly unsympathetic place. Of course, we ourselves had no understanding of any of this until we suffered our own losses. And while we should have been willing to tolerate the clumsiness and thoughtlessness of others, our rage refused to allow us that grace. In general, we couldn't even bring ourselves to inquire about the well-being of others. We just didn't care.

*Maddy: "They want to talk about what they saw at the movies, and all we want to talk about is our children and our pain."*

*Carol: "They ask, 'How are you?' That becomes a problem."*

*Phyllis: "We pick on different people at whom to direct our anger and our rage. It might be the doctor, it might be God, it might be the checkout girl at the supermarket."*

*Barbara E.: "I didn't want anybody from my previous life to come with me into this life because my connection to them was usually through our children, and I didn't want to hear about their children."*

Carol: *"I found it painful to get together with family. It was easier to be with friends and to go places where Lisa didn't go. If it was a family gathering or a place where she should have been, that was very hard to take."*

Ariella: *"My family wouldn't talk about Michael. It was as though he never existed. It was and remains very painful."*

Rita: *"I couldn't stand being around intact families, only fractured families. Their wholeness brought me pain. What they had was taken from me."*

Lorenza: *"Some of my old friends stayed away and I can't forgive them for that. Others became my best friends at that time. I wanted to say to them, 'If you really love me, mention my child's name.'"*

Phyllis: *"Wherever I went, I told people about Andrea's death. It was my badge; it became my identity."*

Barbara G.: *"People would say, 'Have a good day,' and I wanted to hit them."*

Audrey: *"I would pray people wouldn't say good morning to me. I didn't know how to respond."*

Rita: *"Physical contact like hugs seemed more appropriate than conversation."*

Our closest relationships, those with our husbands and our other children, underwent drastic changes in that first year, and those changes continue to happen, even as the years accumulate. No matter how long they have been married to one another, no two individuals grieve in the same way. With both partners so vulnerable and busy dealing with their own misery, it was difficult to lend support to one another. Marriages were stretched to the very limits. In our cases, all nine marriages survived, though we know of others that did not. Then, too, our relationships with our surviving children underwent earthshaking changes that we never would or could have foreseen in our "before" life. Both of these areas—marriage and surviving children—are discussed at length in subsequent chapters.

In that first year, we were consumed with the need to read about death. However, we all know of bereaved parents who could not muster enough concentration to read anything at all in those early months. As for us, we read, no matter how maudlin the material we chose.

*Barbara E.: "I read the obituaries every day; maybe I was looking for young people who died as Brian had died. I searched for books with unhappy endings; they seemed truer to life."*

We spent a great deal of time reading about NDEs—near-death experiences—in hopes that they'd shed some light on how our children felt in their last moments of life and how they are faring in the afterlife . . . if there is such a thing. We thrive on descriptions written by people who came close to dying, and who describe entering a tunnel and meeting family and friends who have already died. We need to know how our children felt in those last moments, and we need to know that they are okay.

We hold fast to the recollections of our children's last moments on earth. From the day they died, we have searched for the true meaning of those extraordinary moments. We will continue to do so until we meet them again and have the answers we seek. Meanwhile, we read and we keep our own journals, hoping in some way that our writings will connect us to our children.

*Ariella: "Our children have experienced something we have yet to experience. They died before us. We have a need to know what they now know."*

*Lorenza: "I call it an 'umbilical cord reaction.' I want to know: What was he thinking? Did he see it coming? Was he aware? The pain he felt was connected to my body."*

*Barbara E.: "I was with Brian in those moments of his death. I had a sense he was someplace else. It was comforting. It stopped me from becoming hysterical. Now, years later, I want to know where he is."*

*Phyllis: "Andrea was still alive when we got to the hospital. I held her hand. I think she waited for me to come."*

*Rita: "I didn't want Michael to be afraid. He was out of control, driving toward a pole. I belonged there. I didn't want him to feel that fear alone and die alone."*

*Lorenza: "Reading helped me a lot, but only books about the loss of a child. I was always looking for answers and for people who expressed their pain in a sensitive manner. I looked for words that really meant something to me. I carry those words with me still."*

Barbara G.: *"I copied those sentences down. Words to live by."*

Ariella: *"I read a book written by a mother telling of her son's illness and of her conversations with him about death and dying. And that helped me because I'd never had that conversation with Michael. It was a way of understanding what he might have felt."*

Perhaps the most cathartic thing we all did in the weeks and months following the deaths of our children was to return to work, albeit in most cases we returned in an almost zombie-like state. We hoped work would be a distraction, although we felt enormous anxiety and our energy level was zero. Fortunately, each of us was employed outside the home and it proved to be, without exaggeration, life saving.

Carol: *"I couldn't spend two minutes by myself. I couldn't go home alone.*

Rita: *"As soon as you were left alone, it went to the very core of you."*

Barbara E.: *"I went back to work after three months. I kept to myself, preferring not to talk to anyone; instead I cried. I think most people were glad to avoid me."*

Maddy: *"Neill died in June and I went back to work after the summer. People asked me, 'How was your summer?' "*

Ariella: *"We have our own business. My husband got me there. I'd sit and read and cry. He'd try to work. At noon, he took my hand and took me to lunch. We'd get home at two or three o'clock . . . and repeat the same thing the next day. We did that for two months."*

Lorenza: *"I went back to teaching in November. Marc died in September. As a dedicated teacher, I couldn't tell the kids to study and they would succeed. Look what happened to my son."*

Phyllis: *"I went back after a week. I went into the lady's room. I was a basket case. One of my coworkers was so thoughtful. She asked if I would mind if her daughter phoned her at work, knowing I would never again hear my daughter's voice on the phone."*

Barbara G.: *"My father drove me back to work. My hands shook too much to drive. He stayed there and waited. As the day went on, he knew when it was time for me to leave. He could tell when I needed to get away from everyone."*

*Rita: "I taught science and some of the kids were in my class the year before as well. They came to Michael's funeral. The kids took care of me. When they left my class, I fell apart."*

*Audrey: "Like a robot, I got up every morning and went to work. Several times a day, I would feel a jolt in the back of my head, the sudden realization that Jessie was really gone."*

From the very outset of our grief, there was an enormous need to form bonds with other bereaved parents. It took us a while to understand the importance of that connection and what it would mean to our lives forever after.

*Ariella: "You gravitate to those people who lost children in the same way you did. You understand each other."*

Was the first year the worst? We sat and dissected that question and we cannot agree on one definitive answer. We do concur that we were in shock throughout those first twelve months and it cushioned some of the pain, which we later felt more acutely. However, we also know that eventually the horrific pain began to ebb for most although not all of us. Over time, we have been able to cast off some of the agony and disbelief and accept the fact that our lives continue, although in a vastly altered state.

*Phyllis: "We were looking for normal. What was normal? We can never know normal again."*

## MARC COLLETTI

Marc loved the water. Before he ever bought a car, he bought a boat. Any free time he had he spent outdoors, exploring and observing nature. But always he was drawn to the ocean, to smell the salt air and listen to the breaking of the waves. He would say to me, "Ma, come and sit here while I fish. Just enjoy the sunset and the beauty all around."

Those quiet times are among my most precious memories. I can no longer sit by the water and think it is beautiful. It has taken my only son.

I remember when Marc was only two years old. My husband Joe and I had gone on vacation in Mexico while my mother babysat. We returned late one night and the entire house was lit up. There was Marc at the window waiting. He was all dressed up and wearing a tiny bow tie. He wanted to look nice for us.

We could always depend upon Marc to do the right thing. He was self-disciplined beyond his years and he never asked for much. We even entrusted him with the key to the house at a young age.

As he grew older, he was the kid in ripped jeans before it became the fashion; let his classmates wear the designer labels. He played touch football wearing his father's old college sweatpants. Joe cherishes those frayed old pants to this day. Marc arrived home from the University of Massachusetts one day sporting an earring. He smiled at our disapproving reaction and pulled it off; it had been glued on. In fact, Marc thoroughly enjoyed shocking us. He stood out at his college graduation: the kid with a tee shirt peeking out from under his graduation robe that read, "My parents think I went to college."

Marc was filled with spirit and compassion. He was sensitive, spirited and thoughtful, loving and loyal, and always he made us laugh with his biting and self-deprecating sense of humor. After he died, a coworker would describe him as having "a gleam in his eye and laughter in his voice."

Over the years, his pets included a menagerie of birds, a dog, several cats, a chick, a turtle, a newt and countless fish. When our cat was gravely ill, Marc was ready to foot the bill of more than one thousand dollars to save him. He shared in the expense but later he mercifully took the cat to be put to sleep, and wrote a touching note of appreciation to the veterinarian.

Marc's love for fishing bordered on the obsessive. He kept diaries of the fish he caught and where and when he caught them. By 1995, Marc was twenty-five and a marine biologist working with the New York State Department of Environmental Conservation. Earlier he had worked at a fish hatchery, a bird sanctuary and the zoo.

The year 1995 held such promise. Marc got married. He and his bride Kate were settling into their new home. Joe had recently retired. He and Marc were bonding as two grown men, looking forward to different projects such as working on Marc's house. Joe and I made plans to travel to Arizona.

It seemed as though we were flying on a carpet when suddenly the carpet was pulled from beneath us.

Joe and I had been to Marc and Kate's house for a barbecue. Marc proudly showed us his first vegetable garden. It was a visual cornucopia of cucumbers, yellow squash, purple eggplant, tomatoes, peppers and basil. Seeds we later harvested from that garden still continue to give us tomatoes and peppers.

As we left that day, we talked of how much we enjoyed being with them both. Marc happily replied, "We'll do it again." Again never came.

Because I was still teaching that year, Joe usually did the grocery shopping. One day in late September, I decided to tag along with him. As we went through the aisles, I was amazed at the high cost of food. At about 5 P.M., while still in the store, I felt a spontaneous, jarring pain, an emotional rush. Instantly, I thought of Marc and his new bride, Kate. I commented to Joe that I wondered how they could afford such exorbitant food prices.

We would later learn that it was at that very time . . . 5 P.M. . . . that the sea took Marc away.

Several hours later, I sat reading in the kitchen while Joe was upstairs. The doorbell rang. Two policemen. One said something about Marc's driver's license having our address and that they had not been able to contact his wife. They were having difficulty telling us that our son had died in a fishing accident. They told us Marc had been taken to a local hospital. We drove there; we cried out, praying it had all been a horrid mistake.

At the hospital, a social worker met us and coldly informed us that our son had been taken to the morgue. He had no idea how to direct us there, however, and we waited for half an hour to learn the location. We then stumbled in the dark from building to building seeking out the morgue. Once there, we were told we were too late and would have to wait until morning to identify the body. I screamed, I shrieked, and said I was not leaving until I had seen my son. They took us to Marc.

He looked peaceful, smiling as if he were dreaming. I wanted to reach out and touch him but he was behind a glass window. I do not know how we left him that night, but we had to go. We turned back and drove away, knowing we must then tell Marc's bride that her husband was dead. Then we would have to phone our daughter, Allegra, who was away on business in California, and tell her that her brother was gone.

How had it all happened?

That day had been warm and sunny. Marc was working on his house when he suddenly opted to take off and go fishing instead. He wanted to try out a location on Long Island Sound, one that was unknown to him but which friends had told him about. Fishermen nearby and others sitting on the beach saw Marc from a distance as he walked into what appeared to be calm surf. He wore heavy waders, as he always did when surf casting. He apparently did not know the depth of the water there and the sand level beneath him suddenly dropped. Witnesses said they saw Marc being pulled under by a riptide. His waders filled with water and he was gone. Nobody did anything to save him; perhaps there was nothing to be done. The investigating detective said, "He never had a chance."

Questions tormented me then and torment me still. Why couldn't someone have saved my son? Did he see the danger he was in? What were his last thoughts? Did he suffer? Where was his guardian angel that day? Was it my son's time? Was it his destiny?

Neither Joe nor I had ever buried anyone close to us before that time. Now we had to go and select a burial plot for our son. Kate and Allegra worked out the details of the service, selecting the prayers, the flowers and, eventually, the gravestone. The stone is engraved with two large striped bass and the words, "The Call of the Sea Could Not Be Denied."

Later, Marc's friends and colleagues at work would place a five-foot high stone and a plaque in his memory at one of his favorite fishing haunts. They sent us stories about Marc that we never knew. He had illuminated so many lives. We learned that his friends will always remember Marc as that unassuming, cheerful guy who wore floppy white boots when working at the zoo, stuck a garbage bag over his body to protect himself from the rain, and saw the beauty of nature wherever he went.

One of my most precious memories is a comment he made to me after his return from his two-week honeymoon in St. Lucia earlier that year. Joe and I had given them that honeymoon as a gift.

"Ma," he said, "thanks for sending me to paradise."

**Lorenza Colletti**

*Two*

# We Are Not Alone

We are the closest of friends. We share the deepest intimacies of our lives. We wish we had never met.

Even though we were totally shrouded in grief, in the weeks and months following the deaths of our children, we somehow came to realize that if we were going to continue living . . . and some of us were not at all sure we wanted to continue living. We would need help.

*Lorenza: "When you lose a child, you need someone who understands your pain, someone who has been there and knows you will never be the same. I was desperate."*

Several of us were able to reach out and grab hold of a lifeline on our own, others had to be shaken from our stupor by friends or family. All of us believed deep down that no power on earth could possibly assuage our agony.

Individually, each of us made our way to the Compassionate Friends, a world-wide mutual assistance and self-help organization for bereaved parents and siblings.

> *Your pain becomes my pain,*
> *Your hope becomes my hope.*
> *We come together from all walks of life,*
> *from many different circumstances . . .*
> *We are all seeking and struggling to build a future. . . .*

**Excerpted from the Compassionate Friends' credo**

Although the nine of us met through Compassionate Friends, we would not want to leave the impression that ours is the only group of its type. There are many similar bereavement groups, and there are many other avenues of support. Among these are groups that bind together because of the manner in which their children died, perhaps due to a certain illness, or murder or suicide, or even because of an event such as the 9/11 tragedy.

There are also religion-based groups. Compassionate Friends is totally nondenominational. There is spirituality in our discussions, but religion is left to other support groups. Some of us have found comfort in being part of both nondenominational and religious support groups.

The important thing is to accept that help is available. There may not be answers, but there is help. For us, the greatest source of help has come from being with others who have trod the same path.

*Phyllis: "There is no place that a bereaved parent can go and feel as comfortable as they can in a room with other families who have been through the pain of losing a child."*

And while each of us found that to be true, we have also learned that organized support groups are not for everybody. Many grieving couples and single parents as well want nothing to do with communal grief. In some families, one partner may need such a connection, while the other wants no part of it. Grief is a highly individual matter: we never know how we'll experience it until life leaves us no choice.

At first, most of us only reluctantly visited a support group. For the most part, we were not joiners. But none of us has ever regretted her decision to join.

*Rita:* "*I was never a groupie, but we learned about Compassionate Friends and it became something I had to do. I don't know what got me through the moments until the next meeting. I went to all of them. It was something to look forward to, much as I hate to even use the words 'look forward to.'*"

*Lorenza:* "*I never belonged to any group. I always felt I was invincible and could overcome any difficulties on my own. When this tragedy hit, I did not know where to turn; I wanted desperately to find another mother who had lost a child.*"

In the early stages of our grief, none of us was capable of accepting the reality that our children were gone and were never coming back. That they had perished from this earth never to walk through the door again—never to call to us, argue with us, hug us—was beyond the realm of what we could absorb.

*Carol:* "*We were only three weeks bereaved when we went to the first meeting. We saw all these people there and we thought we didn't belong; we weren't joiners. These people were not our type and they didn't have all the right answers. Lisa was gone and they couldn't bring her back. But we continued going to the meetings. It was a place to go.*"

*Barbara E.:* "*I thought they would give me a timetable to follow, that there would be rules to grieve by and a right way to do it. If I followed their advice, it would bring my son back.*"

Being in the company of parents who seemed to be acknowledging the death of a son or daughter, and who were able to verbalize that in a group session, was very difficult for us to accept at the outset.

*Audrey:* "*When we first got to the meeting, I felt like I didn't belong. Who were these people reciting how they had lost their child? This was not me. Please don't put me in their category.*"

Ironically, we know that professionals sometimes try to dissuade a grieving parent from joining a support group. Their reasons have validity, but we also know that professional counselors usually cannot know the depths of our despair.

*Barbara G.:* "*My husband and I were seeing a bereavement counselor, but that was not enough. She had not lost a child. She could tell me I would survive, but I didn't believe her. A friend told us of the Compassionate Friends and I spoke about it during a therapy session. Our grief counselor was not supportive. She felt if I were to hear anyone at a meeting say how utterly miserable they still were four, five or even six years after their child's death, it would only add to my own suffering. But three months into my new life, I made a phone call to the nearest chapter."*

And so, despite our misgivings and the belief that nothing could rescue us, we did each eventually find our way to a meeting. We all came away with the same unforgettable first impression: here were people who were living our very own nightmare and somehow, remarkably, they were surviving.

*Rita: "Walking into that room and seeing large numbers of people was shocking. I thought I was completely alone in this. There was comfort in the sheer numbers of people even before anyone said a word. And you know . . . I was just happy to see they were still alive."*

*Carol: "It was one thing to see them alive, it was another to say, 'Oh my God, they're still coming.' But I still went. I had no place else to go."*

*Phyllis: "My first impression was seeing everybody dressed and looking normal. I couldn't believe they were sitting there dressed . . . that they actually got up and got out."*

*Maddy: "Audrey made the most impact on me. I thought I was different because my son just closed his eyes and didn't wake up and we didn't know why he was dead. I thought I'd meet other people at the meeting who had a reason for their child's death. That first night, I learned what compassion was. I heard Audrey's story of this fifteen-year-old girl and this senseless accident. I went home not thinking of my pain, but thinking of her pain."*

*Ariella: "At first you think your pain is worse than anyone else's. Perhaps it's because you lost an only child. Maybe your child was killed in an accident or died of an illness. But at the meetings, you learn that no matter the circumstances, parents are never prepared for their child's death, never prepared to say good-bye. It is a terrible shock no matter when and where and how it happens. There is no comparing who had the most horrific loss. . . . Each parent's loss is the worst loss to them and we are all in pain. All our kids lost their futures, no matter how they died."*

*Barbara G.: "I thought I had been singled out, punished for some unknown deed, until I walked into a Compassionate Friends' meeting and saw so many, many people. Could they all have been punished like me? Did they all do something terrible?"*

We found that the people at these meetings truly walked the walk and talked the talk.

*Phyllis: "I remember seeing a woman walk a certain sad walk, and I thought to myself, 'I walk like that.'"*

We had come to a secure place where we could unburden ourselves of the things we could not say in any other public place. Where else could we speak the unspeakable? Could we expect a civilian not to be shocked if we told them we went to the cemetery and lay down on the ground atop our child's grave? Could we ask an outsider not to shy away when we said, "No one calls me Mommy, anymore"?

*Ariella: "Where else can the parent of an only child ask if they are still a parent if that child has died? When Bob and I lost Michael, we lost our identity. Our future was shattered. Wherever you go and whatever you do in the civilian world, you are constantly exposed to talk of people's children and grandchildren. There is no place to run and hide. Your feel like an outcast in the world of parents and children."*

Would anyone outside this group want to know what clothing we buried our child in and what type of casket we selected? How could we describe to the uninitiated what it is like to have permanently engraved upon your mind's eye, as if etched there in acid, that moment when you looked upon your child's face for the very last time on this earth?

When we are in the company of other bereaved parents, these are the words that spill from us, providing some kind of a catharsis. We repeat them over and over again as if they were a mantra. Verbalizing such thoughts keeps our children alive in some way. It is as if we are spending the evening with them.

*Maddy: "At the meetings, our children come first. It's the only place left where they do. It's like going to the PTA for our kids."*

*Barbara G.: "When we are with each other, we talk about our children naturally and lightly. When we're out with the rest of the world, people hesitate to bring up our child's name. But here I can say how I envy intact families, how I was afraid to love my surviving children, how I had distanced myself from them as a protective measure. It's a totally nonjudgmental atmosphere."*

Carol: *"We get to know each other's children very well."*

Ariella: *"I can tell you all about Lisa, Marc, Neill, Brian and the others in our group; we cherish them all and for us they continue to exist. That's very important, because as the years go by, people forget about them . . . or they seem to."*

Bereavement support groups are a place in which we are not embarrassed to say aloud that we have all sought out the help of psychics, something we never even considered before our children died. Whether we believe the words of the psychics or not, we have gone to them seeking some word, some sign, some comfort. None of us is truly willing to admit we believe them, but none of us is brave enough to dismiss them completely, either.

Bereavement support groups act as our buffer when words might indeed harm us. We know we will find shelter there from things we do not choose to hear.

Barbara E.: *"We know nothing will be said there that we'll have to protect ourselves against."*

All too often, people in the outside world say things that are inconsiderate and hurtful. We realize we were guilty of uttering such mindless platitudes ourselves before we were bereaved, just as we now understand that such comments are made as a result of ignorance and innocence. But that does not make it any less difficult to hear them now. Our skins will never be as thick and resilient as they were before.

Rita: *"They usually tell us, 'I couldn't live through this if it was me.'"*

Phyllis: *"They say, 'You're an inspiration.' That's very hard to hear."*

Barbara G.: *"And I certainly don't want to be pitied. At the meetings you are not pitied."*

Rita: *"You want people's understanding. But you hate it when they show any kind of pity. There's no understanding in pity. It's just like they're saying, 'poor you.' Are they really saying 'better you than me'?"*

Bereavement group meetings, whether they're organized by the Compassionate Friends or another support organization, generally follow a similar format. Meetings are held at houses of worship, libraries, members' homes, or local VFW halls; we know of one group that meets in a bank. Location matters little.

Meetings usually begin with a round of introductions, during which everybody describes how they lost their child and when.

*Phyllis: "Each story you hear at a meeting is horrific, and some parents can't speak without crying and some do not speak at all."*

There is a need among grieving mothers and fathers to connect with others who lost their children in much the same way.

*Rita: "I wanted to talk to people who lost a child in a car accident. I needed sudden death."*

*Lorenza: "Because Marc died while fishing, I looked for any mention of a death on the water."*

*Ariella: "Barbara and Mike's son Brian went through a bone-marrow transplant with the same doctor and hospital that Michael had. When they came to a meeting we immediately connected. We could share mutual anguish and frustration with the hospital procedures and what our sons went through."*

Some support groups divide into factions such as those for parents whose child died accidentally, those whose child took his or her own life, those who lost an only child, those who lost a child to sudden death or long illness, or the death of a handicapped child, or even those who lost children several years ago but still have a need to be wrapped in the comforting warm blanket of a support group.

While the pain is the same for every bereaved parent, the issues one must deal with can be quite dissimilar. Suicide, for instance, presents a very different set of concerns and realities than does death in a car accident. The list of varied death scenarios is long, too long.

Meetings may focus on specific topics. Sometimes there will be a speaker, or those in attendance may simply talk among themselves. Sometimes it's just sitting quietly and listening to others that helps.

*Barbara E.: "I felt I had to go to meet other parents and find out if it was true that I had done something to anger God, as a nagging inner voice kept telling me. After spending a lot of time with the other parents, I learned they were wonderful and loving people. I've come to believe that good and bad things hap-*

*pen by chance to anybody. What happened to my family could have happened to any family."*

Topics discussed by the whole group might include anger or guilt, or dealing with holidays or an upcoming family event. The conversation might be very practical, such as a discussion on recommendations for selecting a headstone or how to respond when asked how many children we have. Just as there are too many bereaved parents, there are too many sad topics to discuss.

*Barbara G.: "When my oldest son became engaged, I said I couldn't make a party. How could we celebrate with one child missing? The support group encouraged me to dig deep within myself for strength and give an engagement party. It's the group effort that sees you through these different stages because life goes on for your other children. It's painful for you, but necessary for them."*

*Barbara E.: "If someone has something really bothering them, like an anniversary coming up, they need to talk."*

*Carol: "Sometimes the talk is negative; people share negative things like the fact that, despite the passage of time, we still feel pain. But people want to hear even those negatives; it validates their own feelings."*

*Rita: "Every time you say something, you're getting a little more of the poison out of your system by verbalizing that horrendous thought."*

*Barbara G.: "At the first meeting we attended, I remember another mother who had not said a word the entire evening, but she came over to hug me when it was over. I needed that hug more than I needed words just then, and she knew it."*

Even in our misfortune, the nine of us are fortunate that we reside in the New York metropolitan area where there are numerous support groups. While there are bereavement groups located throughout the nation and around the world, there are undoubtedly areas that are underserved. We suggest that any parents who do not have ready access to a bereavement group, or who are experiencing a sense of isolation, avail themselves of their local library. Books can be a wonderful source of guidance and comfort. Although we are bolstered by our group meetings, to this day, each of us reads anything and everything we can find on the subject of parental bereavement and life after death.

We have formed our own book club and, as time has passed, some of us have found that to be more to our liking than regular bereavement meetings.

While none of us knew a great deal about computers when we were initiated into bereavement, the Internet has become a virtual international support network. There are grief Web sites. We have Internet pen pals. We can go into chat rooms and share our thoughts and concerns with mothers and fathers around the globe. We tell each other how we cope, we post photographs of our children, and we discuss their deaths. There are no language barriers when the topic is grief.

After meeting through the larger support group, the nine of us quickly formed a special bond, probably because we are of similar circumstances and ages, and all of us lost children in their teen or young adult years.

*Carol: "I would get depressed and my husband would suggest I call somebody from the Compassionate Friends. Just a brief conversation could get me through a bad day."*

*Barbara G.: "Sometimes you just need to call and say, 'If you don't meet me for lunch, I'm going to be committed. You can't call any of your other friends because they want to make small talk, and we want to talk about our children and our pain."*

*Rita: "It's like draining a wound."*

We learned from each other, watching carefully to see how the person who was bereaved the year or two before us reacted under certain conditions or circumstances. It was a bizarre road map of sorts that showed where we might be in the future.

*Lorenza: "At one of the early meetings I went to, I saw Maddy and she was wearing red nail polish and jewelry and I asked her how she did that. She told me it had been the way she always dressed, and her son would know her that way. That's when I started putting lipstick on again."*

*Maddy: "But I didn't start caring about my appearance right away either. I used to go to the meetings like a zombie, but then I went to a meeting and I met this well-groomed woman who lost two children at different times. And I said to myself, if this woman can get out of bed every day and get dressed, then I'm going to do it, too."*

We fell into the routine of going to a diner after the regular Friday night meetings. It was a way of continuing the stream of thought and the relief. We took less of a burden home with us that way.

Then, too, much as there is the fear of saying certain things in public, so too there is the fear of laughter. Oh, how our lives have changed, that we are reluctant to laugh out loud in the wrong company!

Only with other bereaved parents do we feel free to laugh. We fear that the civilian world would not understand, and that fear is far from groundless. Outsiders truly do not understand. We experience enormous guilt should civilians see us seeming to enjoy ourselves. We feel they must be asking themselves, "How could that be? They lost a child. How can they be laughing?" Being with people like ourselves gives us permission to laugh and to be less concerned about the effect we may be having on the outside world.

Eventually, we found the courage to attend social gatherings, but only within our secure little circle at first.

*Barbara G.: "In the spring after Howard's death, my husband and I made our initial foray into a gathering at the home of a Compassionate Friends member. At first I thought to turn down the invitation. Then I felt I'd just put in an appearance and leave. Then I realized that I was thinking about what I was going to wear for the first time in a very long time."*

One of our first attempts to reconnect with normalcy, so to speak, was to travel together to Carol's vacation home in Massachusetts. We were testing the waters, but we were not yet strong enough to wade in too deeply. Just as people who have suffered an enormous physical wound must do, we had to go through a rehabilitation process, step-by-excruciatingly-slow-step. We were terrified that we might falter at the beginning.

On that first overnight trip, we walked and shopped, we laughed and we ate. Food becomes a focal point. . . . When do we eat? Where do we eat? It was winter and the snow on the mountains and the serene landscape gave us a feeling of well-being. We were secure in each other's company. A stranger asked, "What kind of group are you?" Almost as one, we responded, "You don't want to know."

*Lorenza: "During that trip, there was much unspoken communication between us. We knew how we felt. We knew it was a temporary distraction, but we were determined to live this new life of ours. We are stronger together."*

As we ventured farther into the world at large, we took comfort in each other.

*Maddy: "Cliff and I ran into Audrey and Irv at the theater. I said to Cliff, 'That means we're not the only ones like us here.' And that gave us a certain strength and comfort. I had a better time."*

Some of the support groups with a national base hold conferences and conventions for bereaved parents. Some of us go, some of us purposely stay away. Like everything else about being bereaved, there are the universal feelings and then there are the differences. No one is right or wrong. . . . It's a matter of finding your own way, of getting through the day, the week, the month, the years.

*Maddy: "The convention is a hotel transformed into a cocoon for fragile people. I feel like I'm going to a safe place and I never want to go home. I feel like if I'm a leper, I want to live in a leper colony. There's something about just knowing that everybody there is the same and you don't have to explain yourself or be afraid to laugh. They know what's behind the laughter. I stay in touch with people I've met at conventions from all over the world."*

*Barbara E.: "They had groups . . . parents whose children died a sudden death, parents whose children had been handicapped, spirituality, many kinds of groups."*

But, again, not all of us found calm there.

*Rita: "I found conventions overwhelming. They ask you to send in something memorializing your child . . . maybe something like a butterfly with their name on it . . . even if you don't plan to attend. Once I walked into a room and they had trees set up with butterflies all over them. Each one signified a dead child. It was a forest of the dead. It was painful. I couldn't believe that room."*

*Lorenza: "There are walls filled with stories, with pictures."*

*Rita: "People walk around with badges of how many children they've lost. One had four kids lost at different times. It was horrible."*

*Audrey: "I went once and I couldn't go back. They have entertainment. I felt like people were partying. I couldn't handle it."*

We have come to a place in our lives now where we no longer feel an overpowering need to attend support group meetings. But we go— if not for ourselves, we go for others. Some of us have gone on to hold meetings in our own homes. We are always there for each other to mark a birthday, an anniversary, or any occasion that another bereaved parent would remember. We like to say, "When the world forgets, we will remember."

*Phyllis: "I wanted to start a chapter. I had to travel some distance to the nearest meeting and I wanted a chapter closer to home. I started one and I ran it for twelve years. Truthfully, I might have been giving to the group, but I got a lot more back than I could possibly give."*

*Maddy: "A lot of us feel we have to give back to others now. If I miss two meetings in a row, when I go back I see ten new couples. I don't feel the need to go to a regular meeting anymore, but sometimes I feel it's important to be a body in the room for these new people. They see that I survived."*

*Rita: "I run a group now. It's like the nurturing part of me that died with my son needed an outlet. It's for those who have been bereaved for more than three years. We deal with quality of life issues that arise later in bereavement."*

Then, too, there are all the permanent tributes we have made to our children through our connection with the Compassionate Friends. We plant trees and gardens and place plaques in memory of our children. Typical are the benches we placed along the boardwalk at one of our nearby beachfront communities. They bear our children's names inscribed on plaques and words such as "only a breeze away."

Will there come a time when we will no longer go to support group meetings? Definitely. We find we are more and more able and willing to deal with the here and now. There are other issues and there is a future. For some of us, there are now grandchildren.

Will there come a time when we will no longer need each other? Never.

*Ariella: "We are each other's consolation prize. We lost our beautiful children, we have gained each other. We've become family."*

## BRIAN SCOTT EISENBERG

Brian was my only son and he was my paradox. He liked to give the impression that he was tough, but his soft and sensitive side showed through. He played hard with the guys, but some of his closest friends were girls. Athletic and competitive, he loved all sports, but he was just as content and just as proficient at chess. The paradox continued when he entered college and reveled in being a championship wrestler, but at the same time enjoyed being a Big Brother to a nine-year-old, taking him places and helping him with his homework.

Brian was cocky, determined and strong-willed, and he loved to aggravate people, especially his parents. From the time he was a baby and climbed out of his crib fifteen times in one night, his father Mike and I knew he was the kind of kid who would always push things to the limit.

The first time we went to visit him at college, we spotted him immediately; he was the only one wearing a dress shirt and tie. When asked why, he said, "Because no one else dresses this way and it catches the babes' eyes." Even though many of his friends smoked, drank or experimented with drugs, he didn't feel the need to follow along. His friends always counted on him to be the "designated driver."

Although academics weren't his priority in grade school and high school, Brian blossomed at college and made the dean's list in his first two semesters. When we asked how he managed to do so well, he attributed his success to the fact that he had "paced himself" in high school and was rested up for college.

While in high school, Brian took up weightlifting and bodybuilding. He was quite impressed with the results and had trouble passing his reflection in a mirror without admiring himself. Oh, to see that reflection again.

From his early childhood on, Brian had a motto, "Never give up." And he never did until some terrible force, far greater than anything he could control, took hold of his life.

In 1995, the year Brian was twenty-one, things seemed to be fairly settled in our family. Brian was doing remarkably well at school, and his sister Sandy, twenty-three, was off in Israel studying. Mike and I had gotten beyond a number of family illnesses and tragedies. . . . Life was wonderful . . . right up until a 7 A.M. phone call on a Sunday morning. It was Brian calling from Lehigh University.

Remember this was a kid who was a champion wrestler; he'd wrestled in a tournament with a dislocated shoulder, and had not complained about an ache or a pain. And here he was calling to tell us he had a sore throat and felt weak. We were half asleep and we talked briefly. But once we shook off our sleep, his father, Mike, an anesthesiologist, called Brian back and told him to go the emergency room.

Again, the phone rang. This time it was the hospital emergency department telling us that Brian's blood counts were dangerously low, but he was gone—he'd left the hospital against medical advice. They were sending the police out to bring him back.

We rushed down to Lehigh. Mike tried to reassure me that Brian would be fine, but I saw a different look in his eyes. I kept picturing Brian . . . the healthiest, fastest, strongest young man you could envision. How could he be sick?

We brought Brian back to a major teaching hospital in New York City for what would be the beginning of many months of medical horrors. While attempting to take a bone-marrow sample, the hematologist stuck Brian what seemed one hundred times. We pleaded with him to be more gentle and to get assistance. In frustration, he told the two of us— in front of Brian—that our son could die that night if he didn't get a specimen. He finally called for assistance.

The diagnosis was Burkitt's leukemia, a rare and aggressive form of blood cancer.

Brian spent most of the next ten months at two different, highly respected teaching hospitals in the New York area. If Brian had survived, we would probably have had a totally different opinion of these hospitals. As it is, our memories are a series of ghastly medical events punctuated by moments of dark humor.

One night, a substitute nurse tried to start a blood transfusion in the dim light. She admitted she was having difficulty connecting the tubing and turned on the lights. Brian awakened in a shower of blood. His dark sense of humor intact, he said if the cancer wasn't going to get him, the doctors and nurses surely would.

After that, Mike or I or our daughter, Sandy, stayed with him day and night. Brian slept easier knowing we were there to protect him. His girlfriend took a year off from college to be with him.

Our conversations were never about Brian not surviving. He was the fighter who never gave up; the one who would win. Not until after our "Never Give Up" kid died, did Mike tell me he knew all along that Brian's chance of recovery was only five percent. It is difficult for me to imagine Mike's inner suffering as he hid that knowledge from the rest of us and tried to buoy our spirits. Here was a doctor who had saved many lives, and he could not save his own son.

When Brian was a freshman at Lehigh, he had seen the movie *Pretty Woman* and loved it. He vowed to meet Julia Roberts before his graduation. When he became ill, his Aunt Judy phoned, wrote and sent telegrams, trying to reach the movie star. One day the phone rang . . . it was Julia Roberts calling. She came to the house and brought Brian a long box containing a single yellow rose. She and Brian sat on the sofa talking like old friends for four hours. He was bloated from steroids, but they discussed working out. He felt her muscles and she put her hand on his leg. He froze; he was in seventh heaven. She was in England making a movie when he died. We heard she had tears in her eyes when told of his death.

Brian was in and out of remission, and his only option was a bone-marrow transplant. He decided to continue the fight and have the transplant.

Just before his bone-marrow transplant, Brian said he'd never been to Atlantic City and he wanted to go. He was totally wiped out and in a wheelchair. He could hardly hold his head up. Well, he took care of everything. He got us a free room, free food. We only learned afterward that he was a regular there. They knew him. He had made road trips there quite often with his college friends.

By 3 A.M. he had won $800. The next morning, he spent $100 of it and I took $700 home. I had it in the house and didn't know what to do with it. It was the last money he ever held. So, seven $100 bills sat in my drawer for six years until Sandy got married. We spent $300 to frame her katubah, the Hebrew wedding certificate. She was thrilled when we told her it was a gift from her brother. We will spend the remainder on our new granddaughter.

During the bone-marrow transplant, Brian suffered 106-degree fevers. He had terrible pain, which the doctors undertreated. They said they didn't want to turn him into a drug addict. We called it God's little joke . . . to take a strong man like Brian, give him a vicious leukemia, and force his anesthesiologist father to stand by helplessly as his son suffered.

For six weeks following the bone-marrow transplant, Brian was in a plastic bubble to protect him from infection. Even we couldn't touch him. We did not talk about all the possible complications or the outcome because we wanted to protect him, and he wanted to protect us. But he must have been filled with fear and uncertainty as he lay there isolated from human touch.

After a three-month battle, it appeared that Brian had overcome his disease. We were ecstatic; Brian had beaten the odds. He had fought and won. Our euphoria was to be short-lived. That very night, he started passing blood and he had to return to the hospital. He spent six more weeks there and then he slipped into a coma again.

On the morning of May 3, 1996, everyone seemed to come at once—his grandparents, aunts, college friends. Did they somehow know that his time had run out? At 10 A.M. the doctor came in and said it would only be a few hours. We all just held him and told him we loved him until it was time for him to go.

Barbara Eisenberg

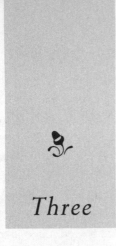

# Three

# Intimacy

The anguish of losing a child pollutes every close relationship. It seeks to destroy our ties to our spouses, to our remaining children, to our parents, to cherished friends, to everyone close to us. Each tie is torn to shreds and brutally examined under a high-powered microscope before it can be pieced back together.

In some cases, the pieces will never again mesh and the bond will break. Those relationships that survive will be forever changed because we are changed. We are never the same people we were before the death. The person we become has to learn anew to love and live with those we loved and lived with before, or perhaps to go a separate way.

The death becomes a giant black hole in our midst.

*Barbara G: "If you take a family structure and you scramble it and a child dies, there is forevermore an empty chair at the table."*

It is a wonder that in each of our cases our families have managed to hold together . . . and not always because of our own efforts at the outset.

Maddy: "*I was emotionally, physically and psychologically raw. So much so that, as much as I wanted to comfort my husband, mother and surviving son, I wasn't much good to anyone.*"

Carol: "*Lisa had been sick for a long time and my life had been wrapped up in her, so that when she died I felt that my life was empty. I tried hard to be there for everybody.*"

We have weathered deep depression, hurtful arguments, separation, estrangement, anger, bewilderment, deep disappointment and suspicion of words and deeds—all in connection with those nearest to us.

We have overcome our own and our spouses' thoughts of suicide, as well as an actual suicide attempt by one spouse and another by a surviving child. We have had to deal with a sibling turning to drugs in hopes of relieving the hurt.

The repercussions of our children's deaths will echo forever in our lives and those of our close family members. The bitterness and the fury will diminish, but they will never completely disappear.

But the one relationship that has never faltered has been that which we had and continue to have with our deceased children. That closeness, which we probably took for granted when our children were alive, has grown to the point that they are forever with us and within us. Our dead children have become omnipresent in our lives. They are the one sure thing. Everything else surrounding us can ebb and flow, change and perhaps go, but our dead children are as much a part of us as they were when we carried them through nine months of pregnancy. We cannot, and will not, ever think of them as no longer existing.

We cannot say for certain that they are watching us from heaven, but the thought that they may be doing just that comforts us and encourages us to go on with our lives. At times, it even makes us feel a certain comedic awkwardness. No matter what is happening, our child is in the room.

*Phyllis: "My son and his wife came to visit on weekends after Andrea died. They stayed in the guestroom. I said, 'Andrea, don't watch.' "*

Most of us could not bring ourselves to have sexual relations with our husbands in the months following the deaths of our children. In some cases, we could barely be cordial with our husbands.

*Barbara G.: "I was so wrapped up in my own grief that it took me months to acknowledge that my husband, too, had lost his child."*

*Ariella: "Bob actually said to me one day, 'You know I lost a child, too.' "*

*Lorenza: "It was painful for me to even hold my husband's hand. The warmth of a man's hand reminded me of the coldness of my dead son's hands."*

*Maddy: "For months I was untouchable, sleeping alone in my dead son's bed and sleepwalking through my existence."*

*Barbara E.: "My husband and I tried to console each other . . . an impossible and futile task. We were so wounded and devastated that we could only stand silently near each other."*

We found we were often out of sync with our husbands. Even if we wanted to be touched and physically comforted, our timing . . . or theirs . . . was off. Men and women do not grieve in the same way or at the same time.

*Carol: "Having a sex life with my husband when our daughter was very ill and after her death was virtually impossible. I wanted to hold him and cry with him. He didn't want that. It took a long time to bring intimacy back into our lives, and it was in small doses."*

*Rita: "I was inconsolable. I needed to be held, to be stroked like a colicky baby. I crawled like a young child into my husband's lap. Sometimes he was there, sometimes not. I had no desire for sex. If my husband did, I worried that Michael was watching. I was void of passion."*

Even after intimacies did resume, there was the nagging feeling not so much that our dead children were watching, but that they might see us experiencing a pleasure that they had never known or would never know again.

And there was the guilt. It permeated deep into our feelings in those early days and months and beyond. What had we done wrong? Why did we deserve to be punished? Could we ever smile again? Would we ever again know emotional or physical joy? If we did feel pleasure, were we not guilty of forgetting our dead children?

*Lorenza: "Marc was married for only three months. I cringed at the thought that I would enjoy a conjugal life that he no longer had. It was as if there was a third person in the room watching every move. What would he think? Did his parents forget him?"*

*Audrey: "At the beginning, I had no feelings at all and later, with the passage of time, even if I felt amorous, just thinking about Jess's death made me feel as though I was not entitled to this pleasure. It didn't feel right."*

It wasn't only our sexual relationships with our husbands that underwent enormous changes; it was the way we spoke to one another, the way we worked, the way we cried, the way we looked at the sky; it was every thing in every moment of every day.

For the most part, our husbands tended to be quieter in their grief. By contrast, we were hysterical. We spoke constantly of our children, we screamed, we yelled, we fought, we cried, we refused to accept and we sunk deep into the depths of gloom. We could not grasp the gravity or complexity of our husband's emotions, and in our weakened states, we lacked the stamina or the desire to even try.

*Ariella: "Each spouse wants the other to grieve their way. Eventually, that either breaks you up or you learn to accept the differences. Even things as simple as photographs. Bob was unable at first to look at photos of Michael, while I needed to see that sweet face and kept photos everywhere. We went from holding each other tight to grieving separately. We had very little to give each other while we were each cloaked in our own despair. We were running on empty."*

*Audrey: "Irv enjoys and is good at delivering jokes. It is difficult enough for me to understand how people smile. How could he want to make them laugh? I needed to recognize that this was not only a part of who he is, but also a distraction from his pain."*

*Barbara G.: "I was trying so hard to be a mother to my youngest son, who was sixteen at the time, and I was going to work. I had no energy to try to understand my husband's feelings."*

*Rita: "My husband replaced his pain with anger. Anger became his drug of choice. As his anger increased so too did the space between us. Eventually, I moved out and got my own apartment."*

The estrangement did not last forever. In Rita's case, she and her husband Tom eventually started to rebuild their lives, courting as if they were dating all over again, and after some time they reunited as a couple. However, they did not move back into the same house they had lived in before.

*Rita: "We had to move from that family house. The good memories haunted me. The walls spoke of my losses and it was too much for me to live with that. The old house was cozy and filled with collected objects. My house now is modern, sparse and minimal. I need the openness and light."*

Each of us today has an intact marriage. Some of us feel our marriages have been strengthened by having endured and survived the worst that life can offer. We have made drastic changes in our patterns of living in order to remain with our spouses and remain sane. We have learned to accept what cannot be smoothed away, such as the fact that bereaved couples can disagree over something as vital as visiting their child's grave. We know that we must accept what our partners can and cannot do, although it may differ from our own capabilities. We also realize the importance of our own needs and wants.

*Audrey: "Driven by a hunger to hold on to Jess and to understand what happened, my husband and I share perhaps an even closer relationship."*

*Phyllis: "Mel and I were like two frightened children holding hands. We were lost and trying to find our way out of a dark place that we inhabited. We grew to be extremely dependent on each other."*

Among the nine of us, only Maddy had divorced and remarried, long before the death of her son Neill. She and her second husband Cliff had been married since Neill was eight years old. So, while he was the devoted stepfather, he was not Neill's blood relative. The stepfather relationship put Cliff in the position of sometimes feeling powerless, not knowing how he fit in after Neill's death.

*Maddy: "I think Cliff knew I had the greater pain and he deferred to it. In a way, we were luckier than the other couples in that Cliff was the stepparent. He*

*felt the grief but it was somewhat different. My former husband and I had bat-*
*tled over many things since we divorced in 1977. When Neill died we became*
*friends. Instinctively, we both knew that to honor Neill and to do right by his*
*younger brother, Phillip, we had to stop the fighting."*

However much our relationships with our husbands have been bat-
tered about by our shared tragedy, there remains the fact that it is a
shared loss. Although it may have taken us awhile to look beyond our
own grief, we all came to realize that our husbands are the only people
on earth who held that lost child with as much loving closeness as we
did and miss them as much as we do.

*Barbara G.: "After many months of different grieving styles, I told Bruce*
*that I would never leave him because only he knew and loved Howie as I did."*

People just naturally seem to acknowledge a mother's grief more
readily than a father's grief. As a result, they often asked our husbands,
"How is your wife holding up?" They would fail to ask how our husbands themselves were bearing up. The same was often true of our surviving children. Time and again they were asked, "How are your parents
doing?"

Just as no one ever prepared us for losing a child, so no one ever told
us how to deal with our surviving children. Only one of us, Ariella, has
no other children or stepchildren. She and her husband Bob have done
away with the traditions that are commonly associated with family.
While those of us with surviving children have found we must carry on
the celebration of holidays and birthdays and such, Ariella and Bob prefer not to be reminded of these events. They will travel over a holiday or
ignore it completely if they so choose.

The rest of us spend much of our lives dealing with the issues that
arise from having other children . . . the surviving siblings, if you will.
Indeed, we cringe somewhat at using that term "surviving" children.
More than one of our children has taken offense at being labeled in such
a way, saying that it demeans their very existence by defining them only
in relation to their dead sibling.

How we address ourselves in our relationships with our surviving
children has much to do with where we are in our bereavement. In our

early grief, "bereaved parent" was our identity. We wore it as a badge; we were bereaved and little else defined us. Thankfully, that has changed with time.

*Rita: "I no longer define myself as a bereaved mother. That would negate the fact that I am the mother of another very much alive son."*

There are so many raw emotions involved in the fragile family dynamic that exists between grieving parents, who are hardly able to get themselves through the day, and their remaining children. The children have not only lost a brother or sister, to whom they may have been extremely close, but they have also lost the mother and father that they always knew.

*Lorenza: "Our daughter Allegra lived alone in the city. For a while she stayed away from our house because it was too painful for her. At times she was unable to speak to her father on the phone because his voice betrayed the depth of his grief and anguish. There were so many memories for her and she felt that we, her parents, had changed."*

In some cases, our surviving children witnessed the enormous grief that enveloped their parents and they could not help but wonder if the dead child was the favored one. Did their parents love that child more?

One of us cringes to this day as she recalls wondering in the midst of her terrible grief if she actually did love her deceased child more than her surviving children. The rest of us do not remember ever experiencing that particular inner turmoil, which once again points to the fact that reactions differ among bereaved persons.

Sadly, when our living children needed us the most, we had the least to give. We are cognizant of that now; we wish we were more aware of it then.

As we watched our surviving children go forward with their lives, we could not help but wonder what the future might have held for our dead child.

As for our surviving children, they, too, found moving on to be rough going. It was often difficult for them to speak to us of their lost sibling.

*Rita:* "*Our younger son, Tommy, left the house a lot. He spent time out with friends and he tried to avoid us. When we asked about his feelings, he refused to tell us, saying that he did not want to add any more pain to what we already had.*"

Some of us arranged for our surviving children to have counseling, and some of our children found their own form of therapy, seeking out and befriending other young people who had lost a brother or sister or perhaps a parent. At home, they learned to step quietly around us and ruffle no feathers for fear of what might occur.

*Barbara G.:* "*My children walked on eggshells around me. . . . They still do. I have not had a good fight with my children since Howie died. I often wonder if my kids think I'd fall apart completely if they were to disagree with me.*"

In the first chapter, we described how we became fearless in the face of danger. We did not fear death for ourselves, indeed, at times we welcomed the thought. After all, we had already experienced the worst that could possibly happen. It did not occur to us that our children might be experiencing those same horrid emotions . . . at least not until it was pointed out to us.

*Rita:* "*At one point my son Tommy told me he would go to sleep each night with a switchblade next to his bed. I think he told me that for its shock value. He was crying out for attention. And then exactly one year after his brother died, he totaled my car.*"

Despite our initial feeling that we could not be further hurt, no matter what happened, we eventually all began to feel the emergence of more appropriate parental concerns. With the passage of several years, we started to worry again about our surviving children. We knew we were "getting better" as such customary worries returned.

Of course, now such worries are accompanied by the sad fact that we really have no control over our children's lives. We want to keep them safe; we have learned that we cannot do so. Their lives are not in our hands.

A number of us were greatly comforted by the concern and compassion of our surviving children in the early months after the tragedy.

Of course, much of what they were able to provide depended on their own age and maturity, and whether or not they lived at home with us at the time or were instead in relationships or even marriages of their own.

Barbara and Mike Eisenberg's daughter flew home from a European trip on learning of her brother's illness. She was with her parents at her brother's bedside throughout the entire long ordeal. She shared every glimmer of hope and every terrible letdown with them until he died, and she's been there for them ever since.

Barbara Goldstein's eldest son Philip took over the care and nurturing of his youngest brother Eric when their middle brother Howie died. Unasked, Philip stepped in and started taking Eric to ballgames and weekend amusements. He had Eric stay in his apartment at times and in general acted as the parent when his own parents were unable to do so. He wore a beeper should his parents need him or want to reach him quickly.

*Barbara G.: "Philip, our older son, said he was determined that our family would go on. We can never adequately express our gratitude for all that he did for us during the early times of our grief. Eric, who was sixteen at the time of Howie's death, would rush home after school and sift through the mail, taking away anything he thought would upset me further."*

Allegra Colletti was working in California when she learned of her brother Marc's death. She phoned her parents and kept them on the phone for nearly two hours, trying desperately to comfort them. When she returned to Manhattan, she took it upon herself to console her father. He was already retired and time hung heavily on his hands as he brooded over Marc's death. Allegra would insist he come into Manhattan rather than let him sit alone at home.

At the time of Jessica's death, Audrey and Irv Cohen were comforted by the love and wisdom of Deborah, Irv's daughter from a previous marriage. Debi was already married with children of her own. The fact that she was a half sister, with her own family and extra years of maturity, gave her a perspective different from some of the other siblings described in this book. Her ability to speak easily about Jessica, and her happy faculty for keeping her own children aware that there was an "Aunt Jess," has been and continues to be a blessing.

*Audrey: "Debi made talking about Jess an everyday occurrence. Each of Debi's children has photos of Jess in their bedrooms. Debi recounts tales of Jess's silliness or funny incidents. They still call her bedroom in our house, Aunt Jess's room."*

For the sake of our other children, we overcame enormous trepidation to cope with social events that loomed large in those early months. Several of us went ahead with engagement parties and weddings that had been planned months before the unthinkable occurred. We could not slight our surviving daughters and sons who had planned to marry before their siblings died.

*Phyllis: "Friends and family watched and seemed to take their cues from Mel and me as we walked our son Barry down the aisle several months after Andrea died. She and her sister Abbe were supposed to be bridesmaids. It was a very solemn time. The rabbi, knowing the situation, said little other than the necessary vows. Our son chose not to include Andrea's name in a prayer at the ceremony, which was very difficult for Mel and me. We were very careful of how we took the family photos. We did not have a reception line. Abbe did walk down the aisle on the arm of an usher, but she collapsed after the ceremony. We all performed like robots, but we needed to be there for our son."*

*Carol: "I have two other daughters. My older daughter Shari was married and had three children already when Lisa died. They were a great comfort to me. But Wendy, our younger daughter, had a wedding coming up three months after. She'd gone through a lot when Lisa was sick; she'd come down from college to sit with us in the hospital. She was terrific; I felt I owed her that wedding. And at the wedding, my husband Don and I got up and danced. It was kind of a signal to all the guests that it was alright to dance."*

*Barbara G.: "I watched with pride and thought of Howard as Philip got married four years after Howie's death. Just before Eric walked down the aisle as best man, I ran over to him and whispered in his ear, 'Walk slowly, Howie is walking in front of you.' Later, when Eric got married, I repeated the same words to Philip, who turned and assured me that Howie was walking beside him."*

Several of our children were already married at the time of their deaths. None left children behind, but they did leave a husband, a wife or girlfriends. For the most part our relationships with these people has been amazingly positive, much more so than we would have imagined possible. None of us has gone out of our way to encourage closeness with these people, each of us feeling that they are young and must get on with their lives. So, any ties that have continued have been not of our making, but of theirs. They have helped to lighten our burden. We know that their lives, too, were deeply affected by the loss.

*Ariella: "Michael had a girlfriend who keeps in touch with us. She was with him for three years. Since his death she's been engaged twice. Life has been hard for her. She tells us, 'It should have been Michael. You should have been my in-laws.' She always sends Mother's Day and Father's Day cards and signs them from Lauren and Michael. It means a lot to us."*

*Carol: "It was very painful at the beginning for us to see Lisa's husband Craig. He would come to family functions. I wanted him there but it was difficult. Where was she?"*

*Lorenza: "Kate, Marc's wife, remarried and has several children. She never forgets an occasion . . . Father's Day, Mother's Day. She sends flowers on Memorial Day to be placed on Marc's grave. On the anniversary of his death, she and her family come to New York from Massachusetts. They go to the cemetery with Marc's friends and then everybody comes to our house for lunch. Her husband comes along. I think he is a very special man."*

In one case, a relationship was severed not by the girlfriend but by her parents. Brian Eisenberg's girlfriend left college to be at his bedside throughout his illness. She stayed with Barbara and Michael for six weeks following Brian's death. When it was time for Brian's gravestone to be unveiled, the young woman's father phoned to say she would not be coming, that it was time to break the connection. His concern for his daughter's welfare is quite understandable.

And then, of course, there are our parents. Their suffering is double-fold. They grieve not only for the grandchild they lost, but they grieve for us, their own children whom they see in torment.

*Rita: "Our parents cried for their children and their grandchildren."*

As in all families, our relationships with our own parents differ from case to case. Some of us, frankly, found our parents to be a burden. More than one of us had to contend with a mother who seemed to feel that the loss of her grandchild was "all about her," that it weighed more heavily upon her than on anyone else.

Others of us enjoy an enormous closeness with our parents and have found them to be a great solace during our ordeal.

*Barbara E.: "My parents were there for Mike and me and Brian, both physically and emotionally. They flew up from Florida and were with Brian almost every day."*

*Barbara G.: "In a book I prepared about Howie for an unveiling we never had, I thanked my parents for giving me life not once but twice. They suffered along with me, and with the wisdom of their years looked ahead to the future and tried to keep me alive to enjoy whatever lay ahead. I did not always agree with them as they spoke of grandchildren and graduations to look forward to . . . but they were there for me and for their other grandsons."*

*Lorenza: "Both my husband and I had parents at the time. They felt the loss tremendously. Marc was very close with his grandparents. Thank God my father had Alzheimer's disease. I was praying I would get Alzheimer's at the time. I would cry and my father would ask me why I was crying. He remembered Marc only as 'that nice boy that lived over there.' "*

*Maddy: "My mother was sitting next to Neill on the bus. They both fell asleep. She woke up and he didn't. She went into shock. She feels more guilt than the rest of us."*

*Ariella: "My father died of a broken heart. He kept saying it should have been him and not Michael. When my father was in intensive care, he looked up at the ceiling and he said he saw Michael; he said that Michael looked good."*

The death of our children has had its affect on our grandchildren, even those who were not yet born at the time.

*Barbara G.: "We wanted a grandson to be named after Howie, but our eldest son Philip just could not do it. Within a short time, however, the little one . . . with whom I am totally besotted . . . developed a stubborn streak. We see a touch of his Uncle Howie there."*

*Phyllis: "When my daughter became a mother, she had a hard time letting sher children go on field trips or ride in a car with anyone else. She would accompany them. She felt uncomfortable when they left for school on the bus."*

*Carol: "Lisa died on a respirator and when her sister had her first child she named her after Lisa. Hannah Lisa was born six weeks early and so she came in on a respirator. I went into the nursery and when I touched her hand and said her name she responded to me right away . . . like she knew me, like Lisa was inside her. And she looks so much like Lisa."*

*Phyllis: "Two of my granddaughters are named after Andrea. That was very hard. When my first granddaughter was born four years after Andrea died, I couldn't go to the hospital, I was like lead. I somehow thought I was going to go and see Andrea. Months later, when my second granddaughter was born, I went and it was easier."*

Our children's aunts and uncles and the parents of their own close friends will always be affected by what happened. They will, for instance, forever panic when a daughter or son is late in arriving home. Death causes a ripple effect far beyond our own households.

Rita's brother Frank Rizzello chanced upon the accident scene in which Michael was killed. He saw the high-intensity lights and made a turnaround, drawn for reasons beyond his understanding to the death scene. He did not realize that he was witnessing the final moments in the life of his beloved nephew, but he stood and prayed as Michael's body was extricated from the wreckage. Later he would write a poem about it, part of which is excerpted here:

*I prayed for you and stayed by you*
*Not knowing who you were.*
*Destiny and eternal love led me to you in your final hour*
*And I could not leave you.*
*You were not alone, Michael,*
*You were not alone.*

**Frank Rizzello**

It remains a comfort all these years later to Rita and her husband that, while fate did not allow them to be present at Michael's death, his uncle was there to ease Michael's passage from this earth.

*Rita:* "I wish I was there, Michael, the moment you died, to hold you. I would have stroked you and rocked you and held you so tight."

. Many of our own brothers and sisters were and continue to be a great source of comfort.

*Phyllis:* "My brother Joel is extremely supportive. He tells us to this day that we are handling this with grace and dignity. I like that."

*Barbara E.:* "My sisters came and spent time with Brian in the hospital. Now they come and spend his birthday, holidays, special days with us."

*Lorenza:* "My brother Ralph has been a constant source of support. He never forgets an anniversary or Marc's birthday. Each Mother's Day he continues Marc's tradition of sending me three roses."

*Barbara G.:* "My brother was the first one I called when we had to fly to Virginia after Howie was hurt. He stood by us then, and continues to stand by us twelve years later. Each winter now I am in Florida on Howie's birthday; I send my brother a package with a shell, a rock, or something I've chosen for Howie and he goes to the cemetery for me. As our parents have aged, we have made a pact to spare them the agony of listening when I am feeling down. Instead, I call my brother; he is my listener."

So many other relatives—brothers, sisters, in-laws and even close friends—stepped forward and were there for us when we needed them so desperately. We cannot mention everyone's name here, but they are the people that held us together and held us up.

These are the people who went with us to the morgue; they brought back personal belongings from the accident scene; they selected caskets; they phoned people, made food, drove us where we had to go. They know who they are. We know who they are. We are forever in their debt. We will never forget all they did for us.

Well meaning as relatives may be, it can be painful when extended family gather. Family dinners mean togetherness. It is not who is there that hurts us so much as who is missing from the table that is heartbreaking.

Of course, there is always another side and so we have learned to grin and bear it when family obligations force us to meet with relatives who cannot seem to recall that we ever had the child whom we lost. If we can do so without disturbing the whole family dynamic, we try to distance ourselves from those unthinking relatives and friends who cannot fathom that we could continue to grieve even though the time they view as appropriate for our mourning has long passed.

*Barbara G.: "Both of our sons had few people from our family at their weddings. . . . Any family that did not cry with me, I did not want at the wedding to celebrate with me. The list was cut considerably."*

*Maddy: "I made decisions about whom I wanted in my life and whom I no longer wanted in my life. Now the friends I have are real friends."*

If we could, we would return to our former lives in a minute. We cannot do that. Life is not what it once was. But it is also more than we thought it would ever be again.

## HOWARD LAWRENCE GOLDSTEIN

We never really understood our middle son Howie. His life—and his death—remain an enigma to us. With us he was quiet; with his friends he was outgoing. He was serious and yet he had a wry sense of humor. He was deeply concerned about his fellow man. He would give you the shirt off his back or the keys to his car. He saw good in everybody. He was a beautiful young man with blue eyes and blond hair in a family of dark-haired people. When he died, so much promise died with him.

Howie was in the gifted program in his public school, but he was the least pretentious kid around. When he was nine, he came home from a college-level computer class one Saturday somewhat baffled and announced, "I think I'm overqualified."

In high school, Howie was seldom challenged by class work, but he was excited about taking on such things as a fight against censorship. Things were right or wrong, never gray. If he saw injustice, he railed against it.

By 1991 Howie was well on his way. He was twenty-one years old, a senior at Johns Hopkins University, a prelaw student doing an internship in the Department of Justice. He was president of his fraternity and the type of guy that people just seemed to gravitate around. Howie was so busy with his life that we used to say he had to come home to recharge his batteries.

And now we are left to ask ourselves how it all came to such a horrific end one night in October of 1991.

Bruce and I had gone to Lincoln Center for an afternoon performance of *Most Happy Fellow*. Even today, I am struck by the irony of that title. We came home early, spent the evening at home with our youngest son, Eric, and went to bed early.

At about three in the morning, we were awakened by a loud banging at our front door. Bruce went down to investigate and there stood "the other Goldstein." We had always referred to our neighbors at the opposite end of our block as "the other Goldsteins." Our address was not listed in the phone directory, so they often received our calls. That night they received a hideous call. There had been an accident; our son was in a hospital in Virginia. We were to call our neighbor's wife for details.

I immediately screamed "Howard" and I could not stop screaming. I was hyperventilating and retching all at the same time.

Eric, tried to deal with me. Here I was, his own mother, unrecognizable, acting as he had never seen me act in all of his sixteen years. I could hear Bruce talking to someone at the hospital in Virginia.

"Do all you can to keep him alive," I heard him say.

The few hours until daylight seemed interminable. In the morning, we asked our eldest son, Philip, who was living in Boston, to come home and stay with Eric. I turned down his offer to fly to Richmond with us and in so doing denied them both a chance to say good-bye to their brother. I feared having both of my other sons on a plane at the same time.

In Washington, we rented a car and drove to Richmond, all the while staying in touch with the hospital where Howard was undergoing brain surgery. We arrived at the hospital just as the surgery was completed.

From the outset, we were told that Howie's chances were very slim. But, I insisted he was young and strong and would recover. He might be paralyzed or vegetative. I knew I could not have him back as he had been, but I wanted to have him in any shape or form.

We went into the Intensive Care Unit. When Bruce spoke to him, Howie knew we were there. Until that moment, I had prayed his identity had been a mistake, but that was not to be.

We were told to touch and speak to our son as much as possible. I touched Howie and spoke to him and a tear rolled down his cheek. There was so much equipment attached to his body that I was afraid I might dislodge something if I touched him. I held his hand and kissed it; I told him to put up the fight of his life and come back to us.

We stayed the night in the hospital, sleeping fitfully on chairs and making regular forays into the ICU. The empty hospital cafeteria echoed with my shrill screams of "I will not lose Howie."

Bruce was able to grasp the situation far better than I. After seeing Howie in the ICU, he said, "Golden Boy is going to be with Grandpa." Bruce's late father had nicknamed Howie "Golden Boy" when he was a baby. I slid down the wall to the floor outside the ICU crying, "No, No, No!"

At one point in the night, there was a ray of hope. Howie's pupils reacted to light and he pushed away the doctor's hand when he was pinched. By morning, he was worse. A minister was assigned to stay with us. We were placed in a room by ourselves, and I curled up on the floor under a blanket in a fetal position.

Finally, the doctors came to tell us they were keeping our son alive artificially, that his brain had swollen and he was brain dead. We were asked if we wanted to donate his organs. I hastily said we did not, and it is a decision I have regretted to this day. I also refused permission for the hospital to perform an autopsy. At the time, of course, I was in severe shock and the mere thought of anyone touching my child made me re- coil in horror. It is impossible to think rationally at such a time.

We were offered the chance to go into the room for a final good- bye. I barely comprehended what was being suggested, and Bruce and I agreed not to do so. Bruce later told me that his uncle had died in his presence and he had been haunted by the scene ever since. He wanted to spare me that memory.

Later, I realized it had been a terrible lapse in judgment. I wanted so to retrieve those last minutes with my child. I later wrote to the hospi- tal chaplain urging him to encourage all parents facing such a tragedy to spend those last few precious moments with their child. I was there when he entered this world, I should have been there holding him when he left this world. I would later spend a great deal of time in the ceme- tery asking Howie to forgive my mistake.

When we arrived back in New York, I fell into my mother's arms, crying, "No more Howie, Mama, no more Howie." I so needed and wanted to go home and once again be a child in the arms of my parents.

We will never know exactly what happened to Howie. All we have ever learned from the police and from a private investigator, whom we hired, is that Howie was at a party in a club with his fraternity brothers. Everybody there saw him and then he went into the bathroom and was not seen again until someone found him in an alleyway alongside the club. He had no broken bones, no bruises . . . just the massive head wound that killed him.

The police theorized that Howie fell from a second-floor balcony. They dismissed the matter as just a college kid who may have had too much to drink. But the second floor doors were locked, and Howie was found under a fire escape. Was he dragged there? Was he mugged? Was he hit by a car?

If there's been an illness or an accident at least there is a reason. We have no reason. His case is no longer under active police investigation. You hear of cases that are solved many years later and the thought haunts you. We try not to dwell on what it was that took our beautiful son from us.

Eric, who was so devoted to his older brother, later told us he was glad the investigation had not pointed to any person as the cause of Howie's death. He said he would have felt an obligation to track that person down and kill him. Then we would have lost two sons.

Barbara J. Goldstein

*Four*

# Redefining Our Existence

There is the before and there is the after. As mothers of children who died, we are now in the after. We will never be as we were before. On the day our child died, our former selves died along with them. Even if we have other surviving children, we are changed individuals.

Still, not all the changes that have occurred in our "after" lives are permanent ones. With time, we find we return to our former selves in some ways . . . usually the more shallow ones. Beneath the skin, we are never again the same people we used to be. Some of the changes are obvious and almost shocking, some are subtle and occur less abruptly.

*Carol: "For almost twenty-five years, I was the proud mother of three daughters. It is very hard to think of myself now as the mother of two surviving daughters. Lisa's death left me feeling somehow incompetent, diminished."*

*Phyllis:* "I think back to before Andrea died. I was smug. I had the perfect family; three children . . . two daughters and a son in the middle. I had it all."

*Barbara G.:* "After giving birth to three children, my expectation was to spend my later years surrounded by children and grandchildren. In preparation, I purchased dinnerware service for sixteen and made certain to have a dining table with room for all. Now my dishes go unused. My table is empty. There were times after Howie's death when I would open the kitchen closet and fight the desire to hurl the dishes across the room and smash them the way my hopes and expectations were smashed."

Once we were so innocent. We never envisioned ourselves as bereaved parents.

*Audrey:* "Tragedies only happen to nameless people in the newspapers. I could never have imagined one hitting home."

*Ariella:* "My only child is gone. He was my life, my purpose. Am I still a mother? Are Bob and I still a family, or are we now just a couple?"

That awful question, those terrible words, "How many children do you have?" are among the worst a bereaved parent can hear. Am I still a mother? If I had three children and now I have but two, am I the mother of two or three? We know that our identities are forever altered, but what do we say to those who ask that question . . . and they always ask.

*Lorenza:* "I generally include Marc and say two. Once when I was at the dentist, the hygienist asked that question, and I didn't want to go into it. So, I said I had one child and then I felt so guilty. Still, sometimes if it's a very new acquaintance, you just don't want to go there."

*Barbara G.:* "I always include Howie and say three sons. If they pursue the topic and ask where they are I say two live with their families in Connecticut and one is on Long Island (where Howie is buried). Then I try to drop the topic. I have found on many occasions when I have to say that one son died, I end up consoling the questioner. They feel badly for having broached the subject. I try to avoid having that happen."

*Phyllis:* "I include Andrea. I say three. But my husband usually says two. The anticipation of that question is always there. It used to put me in a panic."

*Audrey:* "*Of course Jess was my only biological child, but Debi, my step-daughter, is a daughter to me. So I generally say I have two children.*"

*Ariella:* "*I say I had one. If they are really listening and they are sensitive and catch the word 'had,' they will ask what happened. It just goes right past some people. They never notice. It hurts me when Bob chooses to say he has no children. I feel he is then denying that Michael ever existed. But I do understand why he says it.*"

*Maddy:* "*In the beginning, you tell everybody what happened. You feel compelled, but later on you adjust according to the situation. Usually I say two. If they pursue it, I might even make up a phantom life for Neill. I know that's like denying his death, but it's easier on me and the questioner than the truth might be.*"

*Carol:* "*At the beginning, we were very confused about it. I said three; Don said two. Now we both say three. If we are going somewhere, like on a cruise when we know the question will come up, we make plans ahead so we'll be prepared with the answer. That way we don't get so upset. Of course, when people persist in asking more questions and you only speak about two of the children, people wonder. I try to go on to another topic.*"

There are times when we truly have no compunctions about responding rudely to a prying question.

*Lorenza:* "*I was in the school office one day and this woman was asking questions of everybody. She looked me right in my face and asked, 'What's your story?' I told her everything. It emptied the office.*"

*Maddy:* "*Sometimes I actually tell people, 'You'll be sorry you asked me that.'*"

One of us uses a sharp retort as a cudgel for hitting the world over the head.

*Barbara E.:* "*I always include Brian and say two, and depending on how I feel at the moment, I might go further and punish people by telling them the whole story. Many times I make sure to mention it.*"

It is not only the question of how many children we have that rankles us. Many times we have to sheath our conversations with people in layers of strong skin. When our children died, numb and grief stricken as we were, we took for granted that acquaintances, friends and relatives would be our safety net, that they would gather round us and comfort us.

Instead, we have found that a great many people whose lives have not been fractured by the death of someone very close cannot deal well with it. It has not intruded on their personal world and they can neither understand nor handle it. So, they make insensitive, unthinking remarks. We have grown to anticipate their words and to steel ourselves against them. Just knowing a cutting remark is coming, takes away some of its edge.

*Ariella: "One woman even told me that if she was in my shoes she could not survive. I wanted to say to her that I didn't choose this and that I didn't think I would survive it."*

*Rita: "Michael had a close friend and I was friends with his mother. At the funeral, she said to me, 'I can't see you; it's too painful for me because I have this one son.' She couldn't see me anymore because I would be a reminder of the thought of losing him. I didn't see her for two years and then, when I ran into her, she told me there's not a day goes by that she doesn't think of me."*

*Barbara E.: "One of my neighbors said she could understand how I felt because her daughter was marrying and moving to a foreign country. She said it would be as if her daughter had died. Now her 'dead' daughter has two children."*

*Maddy: "People told me to pretend Neill had gone to Australia. I know where Australia is, but I don't know where Heaven is, or if it even exists."*

*Phyllis: "Someone said that I was lucky to have had Andrea for twenty-two years. Would they have felt lucky if they had a limit on how long they would have their child?"*

Some people tend to give what they can in the way of consolation and then dismiss the subject. These are the people who care but wish we would "get over it" and get on with our lives. Unfortunately, these are our lives and we cannot "get over" them.

If we try hard to step outside ourselves, however, we have to admit that we might well have behaved in a similar fashion in our earlier lives, before we came to know death so intimately.

*Lorenza:* "*At the beginning, you are sensitive and you are needy and you have neither the time nor the energy to try to read behind what people are saying. With time, you tend to give them more of a benefit of a doubt.*"

*Phyllis:* "*Probably our expectations were not real. Should we have expected everyone close to us to call and to understand? Like the occasion of Andrea's first birthday after she died; to me that was so real but to other people it wasn't. They didn't call and that hurt me.*"

While those in the "civilian world" may think we are consoled when they tell us they could not survive losing their child, some of us dissect such words and unfortunately attach a very different meaning to them.

*Barbara E.:* "*It's almost as if they are saying that we are able to survive because we didn't love our child as much as they obviously love theirs.*"

We try hard to tell ourselves that parents who are not bereaved tend to personalize what happened to us and say to themselves, "There but for the grace of God, go I." But, we want to scream out, "Look at us, we are having to deal with this, comfort us, don't shy away from us. What we have is not contagious."

*Rita:* "*To sum it all up, nobody can really give us the comfort we crave; that could only be achieved by getting our child back. There is no solution to our problem. Eventually, the remarks don't hurt as much. That's because we are in a different place now.*"

*Carol:* "*The outside world goes on despite our loss.*"

Of the nine of us, Audrey is most able to allow for people's shortcomings in this regard.

*Audrey:* "*They are not attacking us in any way. Rather they are saying that it is so difficult to even imagine what we are going through. There were so many people who came forward with extreme concern and comfort, people who did find the right words.*"

And, occasionally, comfort does come from unexpected quarters.

*Barbara G.:* "*Many I would have counted on to be at our side did not come through for us. Fortunately, in their place, others did, people such as the neighbor who dealt with the cemetery regarding the vault I ordered for Howie's burial, or the friend who called once a week whether or not I was able to speak to her.*"

Sometimes we feel like strangers trapped in our own bodies, for-
eigners who have to find a new route in an alien country if we are to
find a degree of tranquility ever again. Contentment is something we
may never know again, but it is possible to reach a place eventually
where our everyday existence is not excruciatingly painful.

As time passes, the pain dulls, but we continue to define the place on
earth we now occupy as a shadow life. . . . We call it "shadow grief." We
have been dumped here by some force far beyond our control, and it
means we now experience every event, every set of circumstances, every
morning, noon and night, every relationship, every nuance, every grain
of sand in a new way . . . engulfed in shadow.

*Audrey: "I live with a veil of sadness that permeates my very being. The ex-
citement and passion that used to bubble up inside me no longer exist. The passion is gone."*

*Phyllis: "The view from pain brings an entirely different perspective of the
world. It was easier to live in denial."*

But in a strange way, we cherish the shadow. It is cast by the death of
our child, and it is all we have left of him or her, and so we would not
wish it away if we could. It is now part of us, the person we have become in the after. If we are to be mothers of children who died, we will
live with the shadow, but we will find ways to walk in it, and eventually
be able to see the sun rise and set, to forget ourselves enough to laugh
out loud on occasion and to look positively on the new life that has been
given us. It will never be the old life, but it will be livable.

*Rita: "You can never return. But joy and laughter do come back, sometimes
in spite of yourself. . . . Still the sun never shines as brightly as it once did.*

Before we were changed, we were by-and-large spirited, animated
and extremely active women. Some of us had high-profile careers, others of us were quintessential homemakers. We were active in church,
synagogue and civic groups; we enjoyed a vast range of activities.

*Barbara G.: "I had been a vivacious person. I now describe myself as a flat-
liner. I no longer experience emotional highs, nor do I want any, and I have certainly had more lows than I ever dreamt possible. I am not the person I once was.
How could I be, when I have had an amputation?"*

But with the passage of time, we learned to pick up some—if not all—of the pieces. The deaths of our children ultimately did not take our careers away. Indeed, when we awakened each morning to the realization that our children are no longer on earth, we were saved by having the responsibilities of our jobs and having some place to go.

*Rita: "It is important to have something to do each day . . . to put your left foot in front of your right. I didn't even want to be off from teaching for any extended time such as summer vacation. When you are idle for a long period of time, you can take a thought and go further and further with it. At work those thoughts occur to you, but there's no time to take them further. Over the summers, I'd get very depressed. At times, I couldn't handle a week of freedom."*

*Ariella: "The thought of not working was frightening. I dreaded waking up in the morning and having no direction. I needed the distraction of work."*

*Audrey: "My husband had retired, but he went back to work after Jess's death."*

What we have found in our newly defined lives is that we lack the gumption and interest to move further along the career path, or to undertake anything new and exciting.

*Phyllis: "At the time of Andrea's death, I had been thinking of leaving my job. When she died, that was the end of it. I couldn't imagine going for an interview or changing my lifestyle in any way. My expectations for myself dropped."*

*Audrey: "We can't seem to move forward or to make a major change."*

Our immobility in our redefined lives spilled over into an inability to plan ahead, particularly for the long term. For years, we did not want to think of the future. With time, that inertia has dissolved somewhat, but probably we will always have difficulty trying to look ahead with any degree of certainty. Look what happened years back when we planned for the future.

*Audrey: "The joy and passion of anticipating what is going to be is gone."*

*Lorenza: "You really learn to live one hour at a time. To this day, I don't like to make plans. Everything is spur of the moment. It can only be like that. Even when we made a trip to Europe, it was on short notice because what if I get up tomorrow morning and I'm in such a state that I don't feel like doing any-*

*thing that I had planned to do. So, now we don't plan. If someone says, go, we kind of go with the wind, so to speak. We don't make commitments."*

*Ariella: "When I have expectations, I set myself up for disappointment. Now, with time, I find that when I don't expect anything, I am open to surprises."*

Once upon a time we were rather childlike in our love of life; now it is hard to recall what being light-hearted felt like.

*Lorenza: "The child within me died. Anything a child does—the happy singing, dancing, laughter—was gone. Even today they're not there. I now just exist. I fill up my day with as many activities as possible. I go through the motions of my daily routine. Even my laughter is superficial."*

We carried the guilt of our early bereavement into our redefined lives, some more than others. Our families had always been our foremost concern and our greatest source of joy. We reveled in our motherhood. We were so proud of what we had accomplished, and we were all "good" mothers. How could we be punished in this terrible way?

*Barbara E.: "I felt like I was a failure because I couldn't protect Brian. I didn't want to take care of anything. I even got rid of my house plants. I believed I would kill everything I came in contact with."*

That terrible burden of guilt hung heavily on us for a long time, and only began to abate gradually, as eventually we were able to look at the situation more rationally.

*Ariella: "From the time you're a child, you're told you'll be punished if you do something bad. We have suffered the ultimate punishment. But eventually we realized we couldn't all have been evil and cruel in our lives. Look at all those parents who lost children in the World Trade Center on September 11; they weren't all evil and cruel."*

*Maddy: "My husband said if people were punished in such a way by God, you'd be walking down the street and see kids dying. That's when I was able to put it into perspective."*

*Audrey: "Irv and I constantly searched. What did we do that was so bad?"*

Perhaps the most painful change any of us have experienced is the inability to trust in love. We have grown afraid to feel closeness for fear that the one we love so dearly will be taken from us. We know it could happen anytime and in any place. We hear the screech of a car's brakes, the siren of an ambulance, a phone rings in the middle of the night and we cringe. There is an immediate flashback and our hearts race.

Phyllis: "I'm afraid to get too close, never wanting to be hurt again."

Barbara G.: "I've tried to build a wall around my emotions. I was hurt once and I will not be hurt again. Although it has been years since Howard died, I live in fear of catastrophe striking again."

Maddy: "Being afraid to feel close to people is something a lot of us felt. I didn't like meeting new people for a while, because I might learn to care about them and I could lose them. My husband even quit the synagogue because most of the people were getting older and we were going to a lot of funerals. He didn't want to keep watching people die."

Our faith in religion has been tested and in some cases trampled with the deaths of our children. We each travel our own road in regard to spirituality. But we all wonder what kind of Supreme Being would allow a young person to die before they have even begun to experience life? So, while some of us do continue to attend religious services within our own faiths, we have allowed distrust to enter and mingle with our spirituality. We have too many questions that the clerics of all of our faiths seem unable to answer to our satisfaction.

Barbara G.: "I am saddened by the loss of God in my life, but not nearly as much as by the loss of my son."

Carol: "I haven't forgiven God yet."

Barbara E.: "If you were the type of person who did all the right things, you thought God would protect you."

Lorenza: "Now when I am in church, I analyze every word in the songs. The words are so painful, songs like 'Walk Through the Waters.' Where was God when my son was drowning in the waters? For a while, my husband searched in literature and in religion, trying to find an answer as to why something as horrific as Marc's death could have occurred. He has stopped searching. He found no satisfying answers."

Audrey: "Entering a temple and hearing the music dissolves me to tears. I *now go only for the Yizkor service, which is the prayer for the dead, and for Jessica's Yahrzeit, which marks the anniversary of her death. It conjures up memories of when we were an intact family and Jessie was sitting by my side in temple, her head resting on my shoulder."*

*Ariella: "I never found comfort in traditional religion, but my spirituality has preserved me throughout my grief. My parents lost most of their families in the Holocaust. They lost all faith in a religious God and I grew up in an anti-religious atmosphere, but with a spiritual belief in the world. My relationship with God is spiritual, not religious. I felt I could connect with a higher power on a one-to-one level. I was never angry at God because I didn't think there is a God who decides that people will suffer and die because of him. I always thought that life is predestined and that we all fulfill our destinies. It has helped me cope with my grief."*

In our new skins, we try to differentiate between the religion and the people who are the messengers of that religion. We have found hypocritical rabbis and priests who simply could not understand our feelings and fears. But, then again, there are those who have found a strong belief in God to be very supportive.

*Rita: "It's neither the people nor the going to church, it's the belief. I go to set time aside to have a time and place for myself. And now the stakes have changed. Now God has our kids and I have to believe my kid is okay. It's very important for me to believe. I have to work on my religion. The more I believe and the better I believe, then I'll see my son again and I'm connected to him."*

*Audrey: "I like the traditions, the rituals, but now it just makes me cry. It's a reminder not only of Jess, but of my dad. You sit there and wonder. Did you ever think life was going to turn out this way?"*

In the Jewish religion, the tradition following a death is to sit in mourning, or "shiva" as it is called, with friends and family for a week following the burial. In the Christian religions, the burial follows several days in which friends and relatives visit and console the bereaved at a wake or at the funeral home.

The expectation in both schools of thought is that the bereaved will have opportunity to talk about the deceased. We were not for the most part consoled; rather we sat numbly as if spectators ourselves. For most of us, it has caused us to redefine our religious practices along with our shaken beliefs.

*Phyllis: "I found sitting shiva to be an obnoxious social affair. In fact, when my mother died recently I told my brother I would not do it, and I didn't."*

*Maddy: "Because Neill died on the way to Atlantic City, some people actually thought it appropriate to discuss gambling at the shiva."*

All of us placed great value on education for our children before their deaths. Now we wonder why? How can we have stressed the need for them to have good study habits, to strive to do well in school when it all came to naught? For those of us who are teachers, the dilemma was particularly difficult.

*Lorenza: "As a teacher, how could I tell children to work hard? Why did I insist that Marc do well in school? Why did I insist that he stay home and study instead of going out to play? I see my son's diploma hanging on the wall, and I think of how he memorized and studied to become a marine biologist. It hurts. I have this guilt about how many times I had him stay home to 'do the right thing.' "*

*Rita: "I used to think that getting an education was paramount. Now I wonder why I had my son waste so much time on studies he never got to use."*

Even those who aren't teachers wonder why we stressed the importance of a good education.

*Maddy: "Now I would tell them to go out and have a good time."*

There was of course anger in our new selves. In many cases and many ways, we were consumed with harshness and resentment. Anger was one of the few emotions we could still feel deeply. Often, in our redefined existence, we were insensitive to those around us. We were so wrapped up in our own sorrow that we were sometimes unable to grieve for older family members who passed away in the years following the deaths of our children. At times, it made us seem uncaring and unmoved. Our anger wore many guises.

*Carol: "I was very angry, and hearing people talk about what I considered to be trivial problems made me even angrier. I no longer cared about the little things in life and I did not worry about trifles."*

*Barbara E.: "It took me almost five years to relax enough to talk and joke with my colleagues at work. It took so long because I was stubborn . . . more like in a rage. I couldn't bear their laughter; their families were intact and without tragedy. I found it difficult to be happy for them if they were celebrating special moments in their lives. I did this openly and without shame, as I was trying to protect myself from further hurt. In later years, I felt badly about the way I had acted."*

Phyllis: *"I retreated into a shell and became very cold and numb. I thought my bad luck would continue in all things."*

Maddy: *"I thought I would be immune to any small annoyances. I didn't think anything bad could happen. One of the first things I bought for myself after Neill's death was a blouse I ordered that came in the mail. It was the wrong size. I thought, 'How could this happen? I'm not supposed to get the wrong size. Everything is supposed to be right for me now because of the way I've suffered.' I fought with them and made a big deal of it all. It was idiotic."*

In the early years, redefining ourselves meant giving up all the things of everyday, routine life. . . . there was no longer any such thing as everyday, routine life. Of course, the days went on as they always had, but now they seemed to stretch on interminably.

Ariella: *"How can you do anything? My husband and I gave up music, television, movies, tennis, dancing, sexual intimacy and 'civilian' friends. We were simply in despair."*

Rita: *"I could not dance for years. All hobbies were meaningless. Men's departments in the stores put me in a tailspin."*

Carol: *"The list of things I can no longer do in my new life? I cannot go to places I went with Lisa. I cannot look through family pictures. I cannot go past her apartment. I cannot go through her things. I cannot go to the cemetery very often."*

All of us found that foods and items of clothing that were our children's favorites became terrible triggers of our grief. Because we were the nurturers, the ones who fed our children, clothed them, and tended to their every need before they went away, we were left to cry over a cereal box, a chocolate bar or a plate of Chinese food.

Audrey: *"For the first couple of years, trying to shop for food or clothing would render me nauseous. Seeing things Jess either liked or disliked caused me such anguish that I often ran out of the store. Chinese food, Jess's favorite, has become taboo for me. The thought of eating it without her is too painful."*

Maddy: *"I could not go to the supermarket without bursting into tears. There were his favorite breakfast cereals staring me in the face. The unusual soda flavors he liked mocked me. I bought pineapple soda, forcing it down my throat, trying to develop a taste for it because he could no longer enjoy it. I tried to replicate the low-budget meals he learned to make at college. I usually burned them as I cried, but we ate them anyway."*

Barbara E.: *"I would go to the deli, order a pound of turkey breast and say, 'Did you know my son just died?' I needed everyone to know. At the supermarket, I stood in the aisle in front of the sports drinks and cried hysterically. People would avoid the aisle."*

Lorenza: *"I would see a young man wearing a cap or ripped jeans the way my son wore them and I would go close to see if maybe that was my son."*

The trigger might be anything we connect with our children, perhaps a favorite television show, or a television show with an unwanted connotation.

Rita: *"The autopsy shows where they focus in on the cadavers, young people with tags on their toes. And sometimes they carry those gruesome scenes through to another level—comedy."*

Phyllis: *"I have never and will never watch a hospital-related drama because I see my daughter there in the hospital."*

Barbara E.: *"But I'm different. I love it. I can relate to those shows that portray tragedy. If there's a child who died, then it wasn't only my child who died. I also found myself glued to the television for Mets baseball games. Brian loved the Mets; I watched and cheered."*

The types of shows or movies we do devour are those that tell of families shrouded in grief over the death of a child. We sit entranced; we are seeing ourselves on screen and know we are not alone. People who are not bereaved will caution us not to go to see a certain movie because it tells of an aggrieved family. But we are drawn; we cannot stay away. In the end, we often find they do not really capture the level of pain that we know. They fall short.

It could be a certain sport, a stuffed animal, or going into our child's bedroom that ignites our emotions. Something as seemingly innocuous as a child's favorite candy treat, perhaps those little marshmallow chicks that appear each year around Easter, can send us reeling.

While a couple of us redefined our existence by moving out of the house that contained that bedroom and all the memories of when our families were intact, others of us believe you cannot escape the memories. They move right along with you wherever you go and continue to dwell under your same roof, no matter where it may be.

*Barbara G.: "The 'shadow grief' moved with us when we moved out of state. We didn't even have to unpack it. But the distance has made it harder to go to the cemetery, and that is difficult to bear."*

Each bereaved family has to find it's own way.

*Ariella: "Bob and I now live on a boat. We have found a sense of peace and tranquility on the water. It soothes our souls."*

Songs are particularly difficult.

*Phyllis: "Only recently have I been able to move from listening to talk radio to listening to music. At first I drove blind when I heard music."*

As they did in the early days of our grief, a song's lyrics seem to speak to us about our dead children. Some songs seem to carry a secret or encoded message from our children; other songs seem to describe them. Even with the passage of time, when we hear one of their favorites, we cannot help but cry. No matter where we are, we cry. If it has particular relevance, such as our child's wedding song, we cry. Talk radio saved us in the first year of our grief, and it continues to comfort us. Some of us fall asleep with it droning on in our ears. It blocks out the thoughts that would keep us lying awake all night.

Who would imagine that there are such things as bereavement songs? But, in our universe, the one where bereaved parents exist apart from the rest of the world, there are a number of songwriters and singers, authors, poets and speakers who, like us, have lost a child and who dedicate much of their craft to such works.

*Maddy: "Bereavement songs are the only songs I can bear to listen to."*

And of course there are the personal triggers brought on by the particular circumstances of our child's death. Rita and Phyllis shudder when they come upon an accident on the road. They cannot bear to stop. Lorenza cringes at the mention of the sea. Maddy cannot go to Atlantic City. Ariella cannot go into a hospital. These "no-man's land" barricades we have set for ourselves will likely haunt us throughout our lives; they are too much a part of us to ever dissipate.

*Audrey: "I cannot bear the sight of a jet ski. If I see an ambulance or some emergency medical personnel I get sick."*

*Barbara E.: "I hold the whole state of Pennsylvania responsible for Brian's death. It's ironic though because the treatment he received there, at the hospital in Lehigh, was very compassionate. It's just that he was in Pennsylvania when he got sick."*

*Barbara G.: "We don't know for sure, but it's thought that Howie died in a fall. To this day, I cannot scale a ladder or climb to any height. It is impossible for me to look out from the window of a high story."*

The trigger might be an occasion involving a friend of our dead child. Because all of our children were older teens or young adults when they died, within a short time their friends were graduating from college, marrying, and having children of their own. We learned to steel ourselves for such events. Their friends often invited us to be at a wedding or a christening, in a quandary themselves as to whether it was kinder to omit us or include us.

*Phyllis: "Mel and I went to our friend's daughter's wedding. The mother and daughter danced. It was so emotional for me. Even though we try to avoid such triggers, at that moment I was glued to the floor and leaving the room became impossible."*

In the early years, such events were almost impossible for us to attend, but as time passed we were able to gather the strength and to even appreciate the invitation.

*Barbara G.: "We know better than anyone the meaning of the word 'bittersweet.' It is when you stand at a wedding or a birth and know that a key member of your family is not there to be part of it."*

There are coping methods for dealing with such occasions. We discuss them in detail in the next chapter.

The new people that we have become often decry advances in technology. Those of us whose children died in car accidents have great difficulty, for instance, with the invention of the air bag or the collapsible steering wheel, devices that might have saved our children's lives.

Similarly, we rail not only against the medical profession that could not save our children, but against medical breakthroughs that came too late. We become horribly distressed to learn of a medical advance of today or tomorrow that might have saved our child who died of an illness, had he or she only lived long enough.

*Barbara E.: "I used to be in awe of doctors and think they were all gods, no matter who they were or where they trained. My husband is a doctor. I don't put all my trust in doctors anymore. Brian went through ten horrible months of chemotherapy and radiation. I don't know what I would do if today they developed something that would have cured his rare form of leukemia."*

*Carol: "If my Lisa is not here to benefit from it, I do not want it."*

Rationally, we understand that our views are colored by the fact that our children died.

*Ariella: "I look at the whole medical system differently now. Having seen what Michael went through, if I had a terminal illness, I wouldn't want to know about it or deal with it."*

We don't want to hear about scientific discoveries such as the process for saving sperm for future use. Our children did not live long enough to have that luxury. We will not be able to have and hold the grandchildren that might have been.

*Rita: "Loss begets loss; you lose a child you lose their children as well."*

Our physical appearances changed rather drastically in our redefined selves . . . so much so that we hardly recognize ourselves in current photos we must take, such as those required at the motor vehicle bureau. Indeed, we shy away from photo-taking. We do not wish to see old photos from when we were an intact family, and we do not wish to see new photos that reflect the grief in our eyes. We can immediately tell by looking at ourselves in any photo if it was taken before or after our heartbreak. We realize the years since our children's deaths have taken a far greater toll on our appearances than they would have if things were otherwise.

*Lorenza: "I could not look at pictures. They seemed unreal, as if I lived another life a long time ago. Looking at Marc's smile in one of the photographs taken on his wedding day was like a dagger going through me. His wedding album arrived in October . . . one month after his death."*

*Barbara E.: "I was able to look at the photos I already had on display before Brian got sick, but I was panic stricken when I came across a picture of him that I hadn't looked at for years."*

We lacked the strength and energy to care about appearances. We wanted to be transparent, to disappear off the face of the earth if at all possible. If we cared at all, we did not want our children to look down from heaven and see us being overly concerned about something so irrelevant as our clothing, our makeup or a hairstyle. We did not want other people to look at us and wonder how we could bother to comb our hair when our child had recently died.

*Maddy: "I stopped coloring my hair. Most people, including my husband, hate the way it looks now. But to me, the gray hair and the uncomfortable feeling it causes in others is my badge of pain. Maybe some day I won't need it anymore, but for now I still do."*

*Barbara G.: "I used to dress somewhat flamboyantly. My hair was frosted. After Howard's death, I became a gray-haired lady; no use in disguising the outside when I felt such hurt on the inside. I did not want to be noticed. I wanted to fade into the woodwork."*

*Lorenza: "I had difficulty even washing my face. As the water hit my face, I pictured my son struggling in the water. I could not wear high heel shoes because they made me feel dressed up."*

Our clothing color of choice became black. Even years later, while some color has reappeared in our dress, we still prefer darker tones.

Our newly defined beings have new vocabularies. Lorenza had never before known or used the term "bereaved"; now it defines her. She can no longer say the word "drowned." Rita cannot utter the words "guard rail," because that's where her son's car became impaled in his accident.

Our new selves come with new friends. Each of us has discarded those acquaintances and former good friends who could not or would not deal with the deaths of our children. We have all cultivated new friendships, whether through bereavement groups or among new acquaintances or through the advances of modern technology. We are far more selective than ever before.

*Ariella: "In the middle of the night, with thoughts of my son's suffering going round and round in my head, I would get up and go on the Internet. I poured out my feelings of pain, regret and hopelessness into the computer. I connected with Ann, a bereaved mother from Africa whose seventeen-year-old son Stephan died after a long illness. We share everything and have become the best of friends."*

*Maddy: "My good friends, the ones who pay attention and have learned from my tragedy, are different now with their own families, especially their children. They cherish them so much more."*

*Carol: "My friends from the Compassionate Friends group mean everything to me. I feel because of these friendships I have gone back to being somewhat of a normal person again."*

We have all become totally intolerant of matters of little consequence. In a situation such as ours, we learn to set priorities. The little things we used to think were so important—we call them the "gotta dos"—are no longer necessities.

*Rita: "I became more short-tempered. In the big picture, many things were no longer important. My threshold level easily reached its max. Day to day, I would blow a fuse over an insignificant event, and things that were so important in the past no longer mattered."*

For that reason, we cannot bear to hear parents whine about their children being an annoyance or regretting that they will soon be home from summer camp. Would that our children were coming home from camp.

Just where one's children were in their lives when they died is also a factor for bereaved parents as they redefine their existence. There are differences in daily routine for those parents who had a child living full-time at home as opposed to those whose child was already away at college, or married or living on his or her own. When your child is young,

he or she is home all the time, and to a great extent the household re-
volves around the needs of the growing child.

*Audrey: "You're still doing everything for them when they are home . . .
even if they don't want you to. They are your everything at that point."*

*Lorenza: "It was easier for me that Marc was an adult and married. A lot of
his things were already moved out of his closet."*

*Barbara E.: "When your child is away at school or out of the house, you've
already started that separation, it's true. But you can fool yourself into thinking
they are still there since they weren't in your life every single day. You can pretend
they are still alive. I even continued making plans for his life. I thought about
him getting married after graduation, and I thought about what type of wedding
he would have. How many children would he have? It was the only way I could
deal with the situation."*

*Maddy: "In the beginning, I felt so grateful that he had lived at his college
for five years. I had that break from him."*

*Rita: "Michael was still living at home. I had to pass his ball field, his
school. I imagined I could hear his knees hitting the wall at night when he turned
over in his sleep. I heard phantom sounds."*

There can be no comparison of who has the worst pain, be they the
parents of a young child who died or the parents of an older child who
died. Both are hideous events that devastate those who survive. But we
who lost our children in their early adulthood at least knew something
of what types of adults our sons and daughters would have become in
later years.

*Ariella: "We got a good glimpse of who they were becoming. If you lost a
toddler, you would have no idea what they would have grown to be like. I can
pretty much imagine where Michael was heading and how he was developing."*

But, then again, there is the terrible emptiness that is left when one
has had the company and the love of a child for fifteen or twenty years
or more.

*Barbara E.: "Regardless of whether the child was young or older when he or
she died, the pain is the pain and both are tragic."*

*Lorenza: "Young parents who lost a small child will carry that grief for a longer time. I was in my fifties when Marc died and I will carry that grief through the rest of my life. But, parents who lose a child when they are in their twenties or thirties will grieve that much longer."*

In our group of nine, only one of us can empathize from personal experience with young parents who lose a baby. More than twenty-five years ago, when Carol Barkin already had three children, she gave birth to a baby following an extremely problematic pregnancy. The child was born at full term but with impaired lungs; she lived only a few hours. At that time, doctors opted not to attempt to save the infant and refused to allow Carol to see her.

*Carol: "They never let me see her, which was a terrible thing. I was devastated. The baby had been born in October and for years when October came I would feel very sad, but at that time, you just did not verbalize such things. I mourned the loss of the baby and the life she never had. I had carried her for nine months but I never raised her. I never knew her or experienced the relationship we have with our other children. I did not feel the loss of that baby that I never took home or cared for anywhere near as much as I felt the loss of Lisa."*

We now understand the fragility of life all too well. We value our surviving children, and we want to hold on to them with fiercely protective arms. If we could only find a way to guarantee their safety in this all too dangerous world. . . . That has become our main concern.

## LISA BARKIN GOOTMAN

For nearly ten of her short twenty-eight years on this earth, Lisa was afflicted with scleroderma. It is a relentless disease that sought to destroy almost every part of her body, and at times left her on kidney dialysis and on a respirator and subject to frequent hospitalizations. The disease robbed her of her strength, and affected her vision, her mobility, her breathing and her ability to swallow. It subjected her to persistent infection and made her skin and the tissue beneath it so taut that she could barely bend her knees or flex her fingers. Her fingers became gangrenous. Lisa's death came as a result of the complications of anesthesia following an amputation of several of her toes.

The only thing that scleroderma did not take away from Lisa was her indomitable spirit. Throughout her terrible ordeal, she managed to attend and graduate college, do volunteer work at a children's hospital, obtain a master's degree in special education and endear herself to the children with disabilities whom she helped. Despite her illness, she married and never let her sickness interfere with her love or her love of life. As the husband she left behind said after Lisa died, illness was never her identity.

Lisa was the second girl in a family of three girls, the link between her sisters Shari and Wendy. As a baby, she slept until 10 A.M. and never cried. And, while she made life easy for us, it seemed that nothing ever came easily to her. She could not compete academically with her older sister, and she was never a "social butterfly." She worked hard at everything she did. In her teenage years, she struggled with weight gain. Her self-esteem suffered.

Lisa was her own worst critic. She probably never realized that with time she grew to be a beautiful young woman both inside and out, a dynamic presence whose zest for life left a lasting impression on all who were fortunate enough to know her. We were so lucky to have had her. We miss her more than words can say.

Lisa was the kind of kid that everybody knew. She was completely open and told everybody everything . . . including family matters we would have preferred not to make public.

As a young girl, she played piano. She enjoyed tennis and Little League baseball; she loved horseback riding. In later years, the disease robbed her of all those favorite things; she even lost her ability to hold a tennis racket.

As a little girl, she once told me that if it wasn't for her and her two sisters I would have nothing to do. How I wish I still had "nothing to do" for all three of my daughters.

Lisa was always the one to stay by my side in the kitchen when we prepared for guests. As I cooked, she would hang out there and try her hand at baking. She would read to me. The advice columns were among her favorite selections. Even today, I cannot prepare a meal for guests or family without envisioning Lisa sitting there reading me "Dear Abby" letters at Passover as we prepared the charoses for the seder table.

Lisa adored children, including her sister's children whom she loved tremendously.

While still in high school, she did an internship with "special" children and saw the beauty in each of them. She'd come home and say, "That kid is so adorable." When I met the children I was shocked; I hadn't realized they were autistic. Her ability to help those kids led her to major in special education at Syracuse University.

Our joy at seeing our beautiful daughter off to college was short-lived.

One weekend when we visited her, Lisa told us that her knuckles seemed to be "popping out of her hands." One doctor examined her and found no serious problem. Another doctor suggested she stay away from coffee. But shortly thereafter her fingers were turning blue. This time we went to a specialist and were given the diagnosis . . . scleroderma.

"It's not a death sentence," the rheumatologist told us. He was mistaken.

The doctors recommended Lisa leave Syracuse University and go to a warmer climate. She chose Florida State University and transferred there in her junior year. Despite continuous bouts with her disease, Lisa managed to be active in her sorority and developed many friendships.

She thoroughly enjoyed those years. Today there is a scholarship fund at Florida State established in Lisa's memory by her father, Don, and me and her husband, Craig.

Following her college graduation, Lisa went on to achieve a master's degree in special education. She was the only one of our daughters to obtain an advanced degree.

Throughout those academic years, however, she suffered through so much pain. There were repeated hospitalizations and procedures. At one point when she was given incorrect medication, she had to be placed on a respirator and her kidneys ceased functioning. We were told to "say good-bye" by doctors who did not believe she would survive that crisis.

Another time she could not digest any food and spent an entire summer in the hospital, where doctors thought she might have to be kept permanently on intravenous feeding. For a while, her father and I fed her through a tube in her chest. I remember one occasion when Don literally carried her into a doctor's office and laid her on the floor because she was so ill.

We tried everything to help her, including meditation and hypnosis. Lisa never believed in that, but she tried it just to humor me. She would conceal her pain so as not to worry us. She never wanted us to deny ourselves an evening out or a planned getaway on her account. Of course, we would never go. How could we?

One year, Lisa underwent surgery to repair a burst bile duct. She was given general anesthesia and her lungs filled with fluid. She spent two months in intensive care and again doctors held out little hope for her survival. Again she rallied.

Lisa was all of five foot two inches tall, and your heart could break for all the physical and mental indignities her tiny body endured. She was cut up by so many surgeries and clumsy attempts to find her difficult veins. She was in and out of teaching hospitals, where staff thought nothing of discussing the various facets of her case in front of her as if she were invisible and incapable of comprehending what they said.

Still, she went on to do volunteer work at a children's hospital while she obtained her master's degree. It was there that she became reacquainted with Craig, someone who had lived just blocks away during her early childhood. He was studying to be a child psychotherapist.

They dated, they fell in love and they became engaged. In 1993 at the age of twenty-six, Lisa married Craig Gootman. Her green eyes sparkled, her long silky brunette hair fell round her shoulders, and she was never so exquisite as she was on her wedding day. Sadly, she was ill for nearly the entire two years of married life that she and Craig shared before her death.

There came a time when several of Lisa's toes had to be amputated because they had become gangrenous. The doctors suggested general anesthesia. Don and I recalled her near-fatal reaction to general anesthesia some years earlier and begged her to have the surgery under local anesthesia instead.

But Lisa and Craig were married adults and they didn't need our approval for whatever decision they made. They elected to have her surgery done under general anesthesia. Again her lungs filled with fluid and she was close to death. Don and I recalled she had cheated death three times before, and we clung to the hope that she would pull out of the crisis again. This time we were wrong.

Lisa and I spent a lifetime of time together in the short time we had her. We were like sisters. People thought she was my only child. That's the way it is when you have a sick child.

Carol Barkin

*Five*

# How We Cope

In the fourth year after Michael's death, Ariella suddenly found herself listening to music. Some time after Lisa's death, Carol started volunteering as an advocate for foster children. Rita found new meaning in her life by nurturing her students. Audrey is sustained by giving of her time and love to two boys from impoverished circumstances. Barbara Goldstein sold her home and moved closer to her two surviving sons. We went on vacations, we colored our hair, we began to let light back into our shadow existence.

We never envisioned a future without our children, but with the passage of time we have been able to come to grips with that future.

*Lorenza: "I am learning to cope with my new life. I am amazed at the resilience of the human spirit. How do I still function with such a broken heart? Where do I find the will to go on? Yet I do know that I do not want to die."*

It has taken us years to reach this place, to be able to say we do not want to die. At first we thought we wanted nothing more than to curl into a fetal position and be no more. Life held no further meaning or need for us. Our sons and daughters, who were our reasons for being, were gone, and we wanted nothing more than to join them. We were mothers of lost children and we too were lost.

We have moved beyond that. Surely there are days when our hearts seem still to break in half, when we want to go off someplace and scream or hide in a closet and not come out to face another day. But in between those times there is the warm hand of a tiny grandchild, the unexpected arrival of a sweet bouquet of flowers from someone who is thinking of us for no particular reason, there is an unexpected trip to Italy when the weather is warm and the sun beats down on us as we drive through the countryside. We have chosen to survive.

*Rita: "I am living a second life now. My life as I knew it ended. In order to go on, I would have to create a new life and in many ways a new me. Getting better is not returning to who you once were. You can never return."*

As we said previously, we are in agreement that none of us could have made it through the darkest times of our grief without the support of other bereaved parents. To speak of coping is first and foremost to speak of those friends and partners in grief who have ultimately become our lifeline. We are forever indebted to one another for being there and acting as our safety net. We were there for each other at the beginning of our individual nightmares, and we remain there for each other today as we climb back toward some degree of normalcy.

While most of us still attend bereavement group meetings and keep in touch with members at large, Phyllis has made the bereavement group her own special way of facing life. She copes by helping others to cope.

*Phyllis: "I was looking for answers. I was exhausted, crying constantly and living in a fog. Rage, anger and denial had become my emotions, and everything I did was but a temporary distraction. Finally, I was disgusted with feeling that way. There came a turning point, I cannot say exactly when it was, but I decided to take back control of my life. The nearest Compassionate Friends chapter was some distance from my home, and so I started the Compassionate Friends group in my area. It was the best thing I ever did. Every one of us does something in the way of helping others to help themselves heal."*

Barbara G.: *"I found just talking to people in the neighborhood or friends who lost a child or a spouse was a help for them and for me."*

Getting involved with some group or activity that has true worth and gives support to others has been key to most of us in our road to recovery. What began as distractions, ways to forget ourselves for a while, in most cases have grown to be integral parts of who we are today.

Much of what we now do to assist others we do as a tribute to our dead children. We may not have realized it at the time, but it was the search for a way to properly memorialize them that guided us in finding ways to contribute to our world.

Our legacies to our children include various types of funds, blood drives, food collections for the homeless, support of impoverished families and many more projects that live in perpetuity in our children's names. In some cases, we have given needy children items that were part of our own children's young lives, such as toys and stuffed animals that had been stowed away in closets and attics. A great many of our causes seem to focus directly on the well-being of young people.

As a group, we donated several trees to a school for the hearing impaired and we placed a plaque there inscribed with appropriate writing. We keep in contact with the school, which has informed us that our trees continue to grow as a beautiful tribute to our children.

Our community has a program called Adopt A Park, in which small pocket parks are offered up for "adoption." The group or person who chooses to adopt is responsible for its upkeep and beautification. Such a project can include a plaque placed on a park bench or elsewhere within the park as a memorial to a dead child.

Your community may be willing—and only too happy—to permit a similar program on pockets of land which would be otherwise neglected and vacant.

*Audrey: "Irv and I 'adopted' two boys from an economically and culturally disadvantaged home. When we first met them they were ages five and eleven. Now they are teenagers. We tutor them, attend their school functions, visit their teachers, take them on vacations, spend much leisure time with them and include them in family activities. People often comment on how fortunate they are to have us. . . . I reply that we are fortunate to have them.*

*"Jessica's death and the remembrance of her life are what has inspired me to reach out to others. Doing something meaningful in her name has helped me to redefine my life. On the way to the cemetery there is a sign that reads, 'We never stand so tall as when we stoop to help a child.' It is an anonymous quote, and people tell me that the sign has stood there for many years. But I like to believe that Jess put it there because I never noticed it before when I was visiting the graves of other relatives."*

*Maddy: "Because Neill's years at Rensselaer Polytechnic Institute were the best of his life, we established the Neill S. Perri Memorial Scholarship there. We asked friends and relatives for contributions in lieu of flowers for his funeral. The fund has more than tripled and people continue to donate in Neill's memory. Every year an engineering student at RPI receives the Neill Perri Memorial Scholarship."*

*Phyllis: "We have a fund at Schneider Children's Hospital in Andrea's name and it perpetuates itself. And now our children are getting involved in raising funds from their generation."*

*Lorenza: "My husband and I feel compelled to live out Marc's dream of cleaner waters and the preservation of ocean life. We sponsor a marine ecology trip for underprivileged children in the hope of fostering their love for marine life."*

*Barbara E.: "For three years we left the door to Brian's bedroom shut. It was like a shrine. Then one day a colleague was holding a clothing drive for earthquake victims in South America. I forced myself to clean out most of Brian's clothes. It was terribly painful, but I was doing it for someone else who was suffering and that made it okay."*

A friend of Lorenza's urged her to attend a doll-making class to take her mind off Marc's death. Today, as a result of that class and as a tribute to Marc, Lorenza makes soft, stuffed dolls with outfits and presents them to relatives and to needy and sick children.

During his short life, both on his own and with his fraternity, Howie worked to provide meals for the homeless and hungry. After his death, friends of Howard Goldstein established The Howie Fund as a memorial to him. Today The Howie Fund is being carried forth by the Goldstein family. They raise monies to be given to charitable causes, particularly those that work to feed hungry children.

At the beginning of our transition days, some of us ran too quickly, trying to get away from something which offered no escape. We were in fast forward and afraid to slow down for fear the pain would overtake us. We had to learn to moderate our lives or we would make ourselves sick. For a while we worked too hard, sometimes even laughed too loudly. We were off-kilter; our raw feelings kept spilling out and we were exhausting ourselves. But, with time, we learned to pace ourselves.

*Rita: "I lost myself in my work and, at the beginning, I was exhausted but I just kept going. My students became my focus; that's all I did. I knew to survive I would have to find new meaning and to me it was these kids. I did shows and fairs with them, started a student business, and my students excelled, won awards and competitions. I was involved in their lives and it mattered. My life found meaning again. Slowly, the nurturing part of me was reinvested in my work . . . and eventually I learned to stop running in fast forward."*

We found that reading and writing were a catharsis. We created a reading club and a writing group wherein we could share our grief and our recovery. We have wonderful discussions and we bounce ideas off one another. Of course, these are ideas which might seem maudlin to the average reader, but we are our own special type of book club with our own unique needs and desires.

*Ariella: "In the beginning, I only wanted to read anything to do with death, afterlife and spirituality."*

*Barbara E.: "I needed books in which a child died."*

We find we can often write what we cannot verbalize. Writing can be an outlet for the jumble of feelings and emotions that build up within us and need to be let out. Often we write to our children to provide ourselves with yet another outlet for our jumbled feelings and emotions.

## To My Daughter Andrea

*I can talk to you, be inspired by you, I can laugh with you, I can walk with you, I can remember you, I can learn from you, I can hear you, I cannot see you, I cannot touch you, I cannot hug you, I cannot kiss you.*

**Phyllis Levine**

## A Simple Wish

*Sometimes now I like to be alone. I sit quietly and I feel I am with him.*
*I see his face, I hear his voice, I remember his laughter and recall his*
*Excitement and his joy of life . . . I miss him so much.*
*I don't cry as much lately, but when I do, I cry for what he has lost.*
*He loved life. He was sensitive and compassionate.*
*He was kind and loving. He had so much to live for.*
*Feelings of deep pain, emptiness, lack of true peace and tranquility are*
*with me now always.*
*Oh, how I wish I could see him again. Just one embrace.*

**Lorenza Colletti**

## To Howard on His Twenty-Fourth Birthday

*I am the keeper of the flame*
*When others hesitate to . . .*
*I say your name.*
*I am the teller of the tale*
*Words spoken calmly*
*While inside I wail.*
*My tears are a stream in which memories swim*
*While I have breath*
*Your light will not dim.*
*For some it is hard to speak of you*

*For me it is hard not to.*
*I am the keeper of the flame*
*I never hesitate to say your name.*

**Barbara Goldstein**

## Sleepwalking

*Some nights I feel compelled to sleep in your bed.*
*Your pajamas are just as you left them, next to your pillows.*
*I haven't laundered them;*
*You had worn them only once before you died.*
*At first I believed that if I left your pajamas on your bed,*
*folded neatly,*
*You would come home and put them on.*
*Some nights, I could swear that you are home.*
*I breathlessly approach the doorway to your room,*
*half expecting, half hoping to find you there.*
*I am always disappointed.*
*I lie down on your bed, weeping silently,*
*filling the cold sheets with the warmth of life,*
*even as the warmth of life no longer fills you, my son.*

**Madelaine Perri Kasden**

## Full Circle

*Within my womb you stirred and we were one*
*One day an empty cradle, the next a miracle it held.*
*My existence forever changed, a mother I had become*
*Great joy and love unsurpassed in life*
*I cared for you and held you close my precious one*
*The years passed swiftly and I sighed when you finished your teens*
*A man now, how I burst with pride as I watched from afar . . . who knew?*

*But the cradle is empty again and so am I*
*My son, my son*
*My heart is ripped apart, my senses scream for you*
*No where to be found*
*The darkness is intolerable, the shadows engulf me*
*My existence forever changed again—full circle we have come*
*Now again within me you dwell and forever we are one.*

Rita Volpe

We have found that in our writings we give voice to emotions and thoughts that the non-bereaved rarely consider. As bereaved, we share the knowledge that parents have no real control over their children's lives. In writing about that fact, we have gained strength and compassion.

Along with speaking to our children through our writings, most of us have tried to communicate with them through psychics with mixed results. As we noted earlier, none of us wants to say straight out that psychics do not have the power to communicate with the beyond. We would like desperately to believe they do have that ability, and we don't want to jeopardize any possibility that they might be able to put us in touch with our children.

*Ariella: "I went to a psychic three weeks after Michael passed. It was very emotional and cathartic. I felt as though I connected and had a conversation with him. I felt he was okay and, most important, that he existed somewhere. As years passed, I began to doubt the ability of the psychics, but I do believe I can communicate with Michael myself."*

*Lorenza: "Psychics tell you everything is okay, that your child wants you to go on with your life."*

*Audrey: "I never went to a psychic but I wanted to. I contacted one, but you had to call him at a certain time, and then the line was always busy. Still, I think there's something to it. My husband went and he thought the psychic touched on a lot of different things and knew a lot. The psychic talked of a younger brother my husband lost."*

*Maddy:* "*Some of the psychics hit on things which I have no way of know-ing how they knew. I went through two years in which I was convinced Neill died of Marfan's syndrome, although the doctors said that wasn't so. Lincoln supposedly had Marfan's syndrome, and it was thought he might have died of that had he not been shot. And the psychic asked me, 'Why is Lincoln so impor-tant to you?' Another psychic knew the name of a jeweler I was thinking of con-tacting.*"

*Barbara G.:* "*We had two very good experiences with psychics who knew much about us and about Howie. It brought us comfort and helped us to believe that our child exists in some realm somewhere, that he is aware of what is hap-pening to us here and will be there for a reunion with us someday. I recall Bruce's comment when we were driving home after one of our meetings with a psychic, 'What a hell of a way to have to speak to your kid.'*"

Others of us, try as we might to believe, are totally unconvinced.

*Barbara E.:* "*We went to three of them. I found you have to give them the right cues. One psychic we sat down with was spurting out all sorts of things. As soon as he saw a little reaction, that's where he went. So, I sat with no expres-sion. First he said he saw a young woman walking in. I told him I had lost a son. So he said the young woman was leading a young man. Another psychic didn't know we were Jewish. He told me he could hear my son telling me to put the painting of the Virgin Mary back over my bed.*"

We keep photos of our dead children with us each day as well as tal-ismans of our children. We do not broadcast it, but we each have some-thing of our child with us as we go about our daily lives. Whether it be a piece of jewelry, an article of clothing, or something symbolic about their lives, it is with us and it comforts us. No one else need know . . . so long as we know.

Rita wears Michael's bracelet. Because Lorenza's son Marc so loved fishing and died on the water, she wears a pendant that's embedded with one of her son's fishing lures. She doesn't discuss it with anyone; it's just part of her daily attire.

*Lorenza:* "*I wondered what to do with his clothes. Eventually I made a quilt with different patches of his clothing.*"

*Audrey:* "*I used to wear one of Jess's necklaces until it broke. Now I carry her key chain and I wear the same perfume she wore. I buy bottles and bottles of it and wherever I go, I wear it. People sometimes ask me about it. I feel as though I am wearing her essence."*

Many of these talismans that we hold dear are reflective of resurrection and hope, such as angels, feathers and butterflies . . . lots of butterflies.

Barbara Goldstein was filled with conflicting sentiments on the occasion of her youngest son's wedding. She wore a crystal butterfly on her back just above her strapless gown in tribute to Howie. Guests thought it attractive, and only close family members knew it symbolized her dead son.

*Barbara G.: "Such small and inoffensive actions known only to me give me great comfort."*

*Carol: "I have a bracelet that Lisa wore. It has a heart missing . . . as if I have a hole in my heart. I would never get it fixed. I wear it every day."*

*Phyllis: "For years I wore Andrea's bracelet. But when it broke, I did not repair it. It was time to let go."*

When we were newly bereaved we were unable to travel or we used travel only as an escape . . . unsuccessfully. There was no place to go, no place to hide and nothing we wanted to see. And if we did have to make a trip, perhaps a business trip with a spouse, we recalled little of what we saw or experienced.

*Rita: "Initially we tried to run from our pain. We went to Ireland, England, Italy, Belgium, Luxembourg, France, Mexico, Germany, Hawaii. I remember little of these places. Coming back was so difficult. We never found Michael. We dragged our younger son with us and he later told us he hated it."*

The need to try to run from our grief has been tempered with time.

*Barbara E.: "Two years after Brian died, we forced ourselves to take a vacation, thinking it would help bring back some normalcy. We had panic attacks before we left and counted the days until we could come home. It was still too early for us. About a year later, we went away again and began to experience some enjoyment. We still thought about Brian almost constantly, but now they were happier thoughts."*

Now that some of us are again able to travel, we have found the way to cope and find some fulfillment and interest in the trip is to stop trying to escape and instead to carry our children with us in our hearts, which of course is the easiest thing in the world for us to do.

Barbara G.: *"Before we went abroad the first time after Howie's death, we took a trip to California just to see if we could handle the travel, deal with the hotels, rental cars and flights. When we saw we could, we resumed our trips. When I knew I could look at a beautiful sight and not think first that Howie would never see this, then I could go. I take him wherever I am. I am set on seeing the world for him and myself."*

Several of us used to carry along a photo of our child and place it on the night table in our hotel room. We have reached the point that we still carry their photos, but we need not put them on display. We just feel our children's presence and it makes the trip not only bearable and interesting, but enjoyable.

Phyllis: *"When we return from vacations, I bring rocks or shells to place on Andrea's gravestone. I don't need to take her picture along with me now as I did at first."*

When we had to travel early in our grief, even car trips to places within easy distance, we tried to travel only with our spouses or our immediate family or our similarly bereaved friends. That way should some unforeseen sight, smell, event—you name it—give rise to tears, we could return on our own or go off and grieve without destroying someone else's trip.

Today we can honestly say we have learned to steel ourselves against the triggers of travel. We no longer go on a trip just to escape.

Still, those places where our children died will forever remain places we cannot go. We expect that to be so throughout our lives.

Ironically, some of the things our children excelled at and which we were unable to master during their lifetime have become important hurdles for us to cross . . . for our children's sake. These things have become part of our way of coping.

Few of us, for instance, were computer savvy prior to our children's deaths, and they often kidded us about our inability to master something that came as second nature to them. They all would have enjoyed today's computer advances, today's palm pilots and cell phones that take photographs and do a myriad of other tricks.

As a tribute to our children, most of us have now at least become computer literate. We think our kids must be looking down and getting a kick out of seeing us handling e-mail and the Internet. We do a lot of writing to our children on the computer. It makes for an excellent release of emotions.

*Maddy: "One strange thing that has happened is that I've become an expert at arcade games. Neill excelled at arcade games and loved to play them. I was terrible. After he died, I began to play for him. Perhaps I look ridiculous, a woman in her fifties at the machines with children and teenagers. But I'm great. I draw a crowd. Kids watch me with awe and tell me how good I am. I smile. I don't tell them why I play, or why I'm so good, but I know. Neill gave me his gift. I feel so close to him when I'm in an arcade."*

Every bereaved family, whether they have lost a child or a spouse or a parent, will have to learn to cope with the mail. By this we mean the junk mail and the correspondence that continues to come from companies and businesses that have not updated their computerized mailing lists to reflect our children's deaths. We continue to be bombarded with unsolicited literature, advertising brochures and more. Such mailings can break our hearts.

*Audrey: "Just yesterday an advertisement with her name on it came from a store that Jessie liked. I thought about calling them but I didn't."*

You can if you wish call and ask that your loved one's name be removed from such mailing lists. It may work; it may not. Sometimes, the larger the company or entity involved, the longer it will take to get results. Ask for the public relations or community relations department of a larger company, and do not hesitate to express your annoyance. Dealing with a clerk or the first person who answers the phone may not bring results.

*Lorenza: "Clubs my son belonged to in college would call for years after his death asking for donations. I said, 'I already told you my son is no longer alive.' But then there would be a different clerk and they'd call again. But there was a good thing as well. After Marc died, we were contacted to pick up his award from when he helped put out fires in the pine barrens. We didn't even know he had done that."*

Political campaigns can be terribly offensive. A call to the candidate's campaign office that threatens loss of votes from everybody you know may be of some help. Don't be afraid to be forceful.

*Maddy: "For the mayoral campaign Neill got mail. I called up and I was very nice. I told them, 'If my son were alive, I believe he would be voting for your candidate. But my son is dead for years now and every day when this mail comes it hurts me very much and I want you to stop it.' "*

Dealing with insurance monies that came even when we hadn't expected it or given it a thought can be extremely distressing. In some cases, we just didn't want to keep the insurance money and found places to put it, such as a scholarship fund in our child's name. In other cases, there were more appropriate recipients beyond ourselves.

*Lorenza: "My son had just gotten married and he never got a chance to change his insurance beneficiary to his wife. So it came to my husband and I. We did the right thing; we gave it to Kate, his widow."*

As we did in the early days following the deaths of our children, we continue to occupy our minds and bodies with our work. It was then and remains a very strong factor in allowing us to contend with life. Keeping busy is the best way to keep sad thoughts from engulfing us. Although we all returned to work in the earlier years, some of us are now at retirement age. Still, we know we must find alternative ways to remain active and occupied.

A number of us have found our way back to fitness and exercise routines, even dance classes, which we now find cathartic for the most part. We care enough about appearances again to try to watch our weight, and one of us who wore her gray hair as something of a symbol of her bereavement looks great with her hair newly dyed a light brown. While black still dominates in our clothes closets, now, too, there are muted beiges and browns and occasionally a pastel, or even a bright red or pink will sneak in. Color has begun to return to our lives. We think our kids must be smiling about that someplace.

As we have said, we sought out the help of psychologists and psychiatrists, grief counselors, marriage counselors and others. Some of us were helped by them, more of us were not. Instead, we found the counsel, guidance and love of other bereaved parents to be a far better balm than a psychoanalyst's couch. We didn't need to be analyzed, we knew the source of our depression; we needed comfort.

Most, but not all of us, tried taking anti-depressants. Some of us still take prescription drugs for mood swings and depression. More of us do not. It is a very personal choice and, of course, varies with each person's ability to cope.

Phyllis: "I never wanted to take medication. I wanted to feel the pain, to be there."

Maddy: "Usually if you go to a psychiatrist, they will recommend it. I have been taking medication for several years and find it's okay to stay on it."

Rita: "I didn't want to take anything. I thought maybe it would delay my grief and not let me walk through the center of it."

Audrey: "That's what I was afraid of, too. But, I took it and sometimes when I would go to the cemetery I couldn't cry and that made me feel worse. So I finally stopped the medication. Before I took it the tears wouldn't stop. After I took it the tears couldn't come."

Barbara E.: "I didn't take medication the first two years and I cried pretty much the whole time. Then I started taking medication and I'm still on it. When I try to get off it, I just start crying. Being on it keeps me even-tempered; I have more control over myself."

Barbara G.: "I am on anti-depressants and have been before. I tried doing without them and found I could not cope. I am not ashamed of this. Life has dealt us a tremendous blow; whatever I have to do to remain functional, I will do."

We used to identify ourselves as mothers. After we lost our children that identity was shaken, but we realize we are still mothers. And, despite what we have been through, we have emerged also as teachers, business women, career women, counselors, wives, grandmothers, sisters, daughters and friends. We each have our own interests. We look different, we act differently and we think differently.

Once we realize and accept without guilt that we are so much more than bereaved mothers, we are a long way toward coping with our grief. We cannot say we are strong enough to deal with whatever comes our way. If there is one thing we have learned it is to expect the unexpected.

And so we manage. We go from day to day. The transition is subtle. Like the twelve-step program for addicts of all types, we take it one small step at a time. We know we have survived the worst that life can offer and in that alone there is some strength. Let others who do not know any better speak of "closure." There is no such thing in regard to a dead child. You never close that part of your life. It molds you forevermore.

Just as the births of our children made us who we were as young mothers, so their deaths are a large part of who we are now. We accept that. But, we concentrate on moving forward. We have no intention of dying. We may not always admit that, but how else to explain the fact that we go for annual mammograms and buckle our seat belts when we drive. We owe it to our children, both dead and surviving, to move on.

## ANDREA LEVINE

For several months, I had been having fleeting thoughts that someone in our family would die. I tried to put such notions aside, but could not and found them most disturbing.

On an unusually mild Saturday afternoon in December of 1987, Andrea and I went shopping for a new outfit for her. My daughter truly had a passion for shopping. We joked that her motto was "out of the bag and onto my back." But it was not only for herself that Andrea shopped. It was usually Andrea who thought to buy the greeting cards, and it was she who reminded her older brother and sister when there was a family birthday or anniversary to be recognized with a gift.

As we walked, she told me to remember that she was an organ donor. I looked at her and wondered what she was thinking. "So what," was all I said.

That evening Andrea left to drive to New Jersey to visit a friend. Typical of mothers everywhere, I cautioned her to start out early and drive carefully.

"Ma," she said, "don't worry about me; worry about the other drivers." Those were to be the last words Andrea ever said to me.

At 11 P.M. a police officer phoned and said Andrea had been in a serious car accident in Bloomfield, New Jersey. When our children were young, we had always told them to phone if they had any difficulty and when we could hear their voice we would know all was well. I asked the police officer if I could speak to Andrea. When he said I could not, I knew we were up against something serious.

Andrea was the youngest of our three children. She was caring and sensitive with a warm, winning personality and a ready smile. She made and kept friends with ease and was in constant touch seemingly with all of them at once by telephone. The image of her talking on two phones simultaneously will forever bring a smile to my face.

She was able to pick and choose her friends wisely because she had an uncanny ability to cut to the chase. She sensed who was genuine and who was not. She was a dark-haired, cute and tiny dynamo whom we nicknamed "Wheels" because she was always spinning, talking, going and doing. When Andrea was at home, the house was always busy.

She was our family personality and she made us laugh with such pranks as filling the refrigerator with family shoes when she found it depressingly empty after her big brother left for college.

Apparently, Andrea lost her way that December night. She was alone in the car and in the wrong place at the wrong time when a young man of eighteen plowed into the driver's side of her car. There were no drugs or alcohol involved but it was his first time at the wheel. He was just an inexperienced driver who walked away without a scratch.

We rushed down to the hospital trauma center in New Jersey where Andrea had been taken and was already undergoing surgery. Perhaps she knew we were on our way because she was still alive when we arrived, but it was awhile before we could see her.

We sat in a small waiting room hoping and praying for good news. Finally a doctor and two nurses came in. The doctor told us in rambling fashion that Andrea's surgery had not gone well. I asked him to get to the point, and he told us that Andrea's liver had ruptured and there was nothing they could do to save her.

I recall looking behind me to see who else was in that little room because I could not believe the doctor was speaking to us. At such a time, your mind and body separate, you feel weightless. The shock is so incomprehensible that numbness settles in as if to protect you from something too horrendous to absorb.

They wheeled Andrea down for us to see her. She still wore the shower cap she had worn during the surgery, and there was fresh blood coming from her nose. . . . These terrible last images remain forever engraved on our hearts and minds.

It was at that moment that an incredibly insensitive nurse or orderly stepped up to place an identification tag on Andrea's toe. The social worker cautioned her that this was not the appropriate time or place.

Although Andrea had already been pronounced dead, I knew she would know we were there to say good-bye. I touched her and kissed her and held her soft sweet hand. I felt enormous love, sadness and tenderness, and I felt very weak. I do not think I will ever again feel that way. We agreed to donate Andrea's corneas in line with what she had told me just that morning was her wish. God, how far away that morning seemed as we agreed to carry out her final wish.

We left the hospital, my husband Mel at the wheel, his tears flowing. I never cried; I never screamed. I sat paralyzed.

Andrea's sister Abbe, her brother Barry and Barry's fiancee, Patty, helped us through the awful chore of making the funeral arrangements. I picked out the coffin and the clothes that my dear child would sleep in for the rest of her life. We sent over a photo of the family to be placed in the coffin. I would have loved to include a telephone . . . Andrea's favorite instrument.

That night at the funeral chapel we were an intact family for the last time. As long as her coffin was open, I was able to function. Abbe and Barry both eulogized their sister before the standing-room-only crowd at her funeral service at the temple the next day. Andrea was not a religious person, but she would have loved that crowd.

At the age of twenty-two, Andrea was an undiscovered treasure. As we left her at the cemetery, I looked back and saw a shadow of myself at her graveside. I knew I would never leave her. Part of me would always be there at her side. I left the cemetery a different person.

I visited Andrea's grave frequently those first two years. I was obsessed with getting her stone in place. It reads, "For your caring, humor, friendship and love. For this we miss you deeply."

Andrea and Mel had shared so many precious times and experiences. She worked with Mel at his business after she graduated from college. After her death, he could not go back to work without friends escorting him. We were all very concerned about him.

As for myself, Andrea and I shared a beautifully close mother-daughter bond. Despite the fact that I was the mother and she the daughter, she possessed a wisdom beyond her short years, and in some ways I looked to her as my mentor. Perhaps she still fills that role. With Andrea's death, I have lost my best friend.

**Phyllis Levine**

*Six*

# Holidays, Birthdays, Anniversaries

Holidays are hell. There is no escaping that sad fact. Holidays, birthdays and certain anniversaries that used to hold precious meaning for us and for our families are now times when the memories are almost unbearable.

The first of everything is the worst of everything. We all dreaded the coming of the first holiday, the first birthday, the first death anniversary. In the beginning we were for the most part frozen on those "first" days. We were incapable of doing anything, or if we did act it was as if by rote.

*Rita: "At that first Christmas, the whole family went through the motions. I thought to put up a tree to give some light to my younger son's life. My husband did not want to do that, so he brought home a tree that resembled a broomstick with arms. There were no surprise gifts. Our life was in a plain brown wrapper."*

Over time, we have learned that the best way to survive these tor-turous holidays is to develop mechanisms that will carry us through them or, better still, find ways to avoid them completely and allow them to pass unmarked and as quietly as possible.

Unfortunately, our society finds such behavior almost unthinkable. Americans make much of holidays, so much so that we seem at times to slide simply from celebrating one "special" occasion to preparing for the next, and always with great fanfare. Labor Day barbecues have hardly ended and the toys of summer been stashed away than the stores overflow with table decorations for Thanksgiving . . . the family feast and a day of giving thanks. Christmas and Chanukah, the days that brought such wonder to our childrens' eyes, are anticipated with cele-bratory glee for months by the general public. Signs and symbols for those holidays are out and all around us when we are scarcely into Oc-tober.

Mother's Day and Father's Day are their own particular form of heartbreak. Images flood back over us . . . a toddler's hand opening to disclose a lopsided clay heart made especially for Mommy, a small son's painstakingly printed big block letters expressing love on a Father's Day card. Mother's Day and Father's Day can no longer exist for us, even if we have other children.

*Maddy: "Neill was buried on Father's Day. How ironic that his father and stepfather are now forever united on that day by their grief."*

We will mark those days in some way and at some other time with surviving children and grandchildren. But, never again will it be with the traditional flowers, gifts and, of course, the cards for every occasion imaginable that the greeting card industry has plotted for us. Some of us are even repulsed by greeting cards.

*Barbara E.: "I no longer send cards. I found that signing three names instead of four broke my heart. So, I just stopped."*

*Audrey: "One of the hardest things is picking a card in the store. The words mother, father or daughter smack me in the face."*

*Carol: "And those entire family photo cards that people send us. How in-sensitive can they be."*

*Rita: "Receiving cards can be just bizarre . . . ridiculous cards wishing us joy."*

Then there are the unsolicited catalogues that flood our mailboxes: Buy for the holidays, decorate every room in your home for the holidays, dress for the holidays, prepare for the holidays.

The media is our enemy when it comes to celebration time. When the television, the radio, newspapers and magazines are not delivering news of the grim world situation to our living rooms and doorsteps, they are in holiday mode. Where will Americans be traveling this upcoming holiday? What should we be buying as gifts this year? What styles are in for the holiday season?

Everyone is in a rush to celebrate, while we are in a rush to hide from what for others is family time . . . intact family time. We are no longer intact; we can no longer celebrate.

What can we do? We must get past these days, year after year after year. We survive in different ways. We rely on those friends who also are bereaved because they can fully understand what we are going through and realize that the agony does not cease with time. We cherish close friends, bereaved and otherwise, who care enough to call us and commiserate on a particular occasion, or who care enough to let us alone. They know us well and know our needs at these times that jar our memories.

Over the years, we have tried to lose ourselves in mindless activity by running here, there and everywhere. We would go away to try to escape, but cannot find any place to hide from memories. So we attempt to replace the loss that has affected our lives by giving to someone else; we seek to erase the ugliness of what has happened with something beautiful. But it is hard, very hard.

Perhaps the best and simplest way we can go about surviving the holidays that come so often and with such fanfare is to find a way to let the death of our child be a part of it. Their deaths are something we must live with forevermore, and so they must become part of special occasions if we are to mark such occasions at all.

*Ariella: "Bob and I now give each other cards and gifts that include Michael. Bob signs his cards Mike and Dad, I sign mine Mom and Michael."*

We feel and accept our children's presence very strongly on those days. We have to accept the fact that these special days will always be accompanied by great pain for us. We may rail against that, but it is the only way we can endure and wake up on the following morning with yet another holiday celebration behind us instead of looming before us.

*Phyllis: "Rosh Hashanah ushers in the New Year. On that day The Book of Life is opened, and ten days later on Yom Kippur it is sealed. In that time, it is determined who will live and who will die in the coming year. For Andrea, the book was slammed shut. The holiday has become my enemy. I feel I am fighting single-handedly against an invisible force. It overwhelms me. All I can do is pray for Andrea that she is safe.*

*"The Yom Kippur service ends in Yiskor when we say the prayers for the dead in our families. I choose to sit by myself and not greet anyone. I sit and think who I have become. I think that my old-time friends don't even know the person I am now. I do not think about my mother or father or anyone else, I only think about Andrea.*

*"Does the pain get better? No!!!! The pain softens. How do I explain that? You can stay in bed and become immobilized with your grief, or you can choose to land on your feet. My friends who are also bereaved save me at times like these. Our bond is unique. They help me through it, but the best part of any holiday is when it is over."*

*Barbara G.: "I could not go to the synagogue after Howie died. My husband Bruce went with my father. But after one year, he could not bear listening to the warnings of who would live and who would die. It was tearing him apart. He never went back."*

We try to outrun our grief, but it never works. . . . Grief always outruns us, particularly in the early years.

*Rita: "It was just before Christmas and I was continually in fast forward, afraid to slow down, knowing that if I did, the pain would overtake me. I shopped, I wrapped, I shopped, I exchanged, I bought again, I ran, I wrapped, I collapsed, exhausted and too tired to think. I fit in a trip to the cemetery. I cared for my husband, Tom, who was having his own meltdown. I kept running, thinking if I ran fast enough, sickness and emotional pain could not catch me.*

*"I attended Christmas mass by myself and stood alone in a church filled*

*with intact families while shadows of my own life rose before me. Memory after memory bubbled to the surface as I replayed those joyous times. Now they are swords that pierce my soul. The ghosts of Christmases past came back to haunt me. I felt empty, alone and angry. What was it all for? Whose life was that? The mother, the me of that past life, was no longer me. She was calm, warm and soft. That person is gone forever and now unattainable. I am someone else today. I do not like her as much."*

No, we do not like the new people we have become as much as we liked the innocent people we were before. But we have to learn to accept our new selves, those changed, unsmiling on the inside new selves, who are always on guard, awaiting a possible new hurt. We have become vulnerable, fragile individuals. Those qualities now define us. Once we fully accept that reality our lives do become easier. We cannot undo what happened, we must make it part of our new lives.

*Carol: "The first years, I spent a lot of time worrying about approaching anniversaries, birthdays, holidays, death days. I tried to think of different ways to get through. On Lisa's birthday, I would ask my other daughters and Lisa's husband, Craig, to meet me at the cemetery. I would donate blood.*

*"I agonized over not giving Lisa enough time as my life seemed to be going forth without her. After six years, I softened up on myself. I decided these days to me are no different from any other days. Every day I am without Lisa. I try not to pay special attention to any so-called special days."*

It is on these occasions when the world celebrates that we often sit down and achieve some solace by sending our thoughts to our children, be it in poetry or prose. Writing to and about our children is always a relief of pent-up emotions, but particularly so on those special days.

### The First Thanksgiving

*Today is Thanksgiving, Lord*
*And I don't know what to say.*
*On June Fifteenth of this fractured year,*
*You took my son away.*
*Why should I be giving thanks?*

*It makes no sense to pray.*
*If You were listening to my prayers,*
*You would have let him stay.*
*I have wonderful friends and relatives, Lord,*
*Still, it's very tough.*
*I love each and every one of them*
*And yet it's not enough.*
*The pain is unbelievable,*
*It cuts right through my soul.*
*Although my family helps me cope,*
*We are no longer whole.*
*Could You send a sign, Lord,*
*That heaven does exist?*
*Is my child at peace in a better place,*
*Not cursed by You, but kissed?*
*I could give thanks once again,*
*If I knew he was safe and well,*
*And, in spite of the hole in my broken heart,*
*Survive this endless hell.*

**Madelaine Perri Kasden**

Our children's birthdays cannot help but become times of remembrance and reflection. In the beginning, we suffered as we anticipated such days. The countdown made us hyperventilate. We obsessed over how we would handle it.

Even with the passage of time, we need not consult a calendar to know that such a day looms ahead. Our bodies anticipate it for us. We tense up, we grow irritable, we feel depressed. Time blunts some of the more acute sensations, but still the old feelings flood back over us, and we are painfully aware that a day never to be forgotten is coming once again.

*Lorenza: "Marc's birthday was the day before Thanksgiving. He loved that holiday and he loved the traditional turkey leg. I always keep that image of him sitting at the table, turkey leg in hand saying, 'I'm king.' On the first Thanksgiving after his death, I thought to bring a turkey leg to his grave, but then decided against it. Thank God Thanksgiving falls on a weekday, and it doesn't have to be a three-day weekend. On Thanksgiving, many restaurants are closed, but still we do not eat at home. We go out to a movie, we go and eat pasta, anything to keep our minds occupied. It's very painful."*

On our child's birthday, we wrap ourselves in the warm memories that only a parent can know. We cannot escape these thoughts, so it is best to give in and bathe ourselves in them, even as we try to immerse ourselves in our work or our other responsibilities. We try to make the day pass as painlessly as possible by doing things our child enjoyed, such as shopping or eating a special food, perhaps going to some place they favored.

*Barbara E.: "After the first year, we decided to celebrate Brian's life by celebrating his birthday."*

*Audrey: "Jessie's second birthday after her death was the day we decided to celebrate her life by becoming godparents to two boys."*

As with a holiday, a child's birthday is a good time to communicate with a deceased son or daughter. We write long notes by hand or on the computer to bring our children up to date on the family's comings and goings. We tell them of our deepest thoughts and emotions and how we are faring without them.

## A Birthday Message

*I can't call you on your birthday and sing Happy Birthday.*
*I can't see your wish list so that I can buy you a gift.*
*I can't give you a birthday hug and kiss.*
*I can't celebrate with you.*
*I can visit you at the cemetery.*
*I can hurt and long for you.*
*I can think about you.*
*I can share my sadness with whoever calls.*
*I want to do what I cannot and not what I can.*

*I love you Andrea.*

*Happy Birthday*

                                            Ma (Phyllis Levine)

We find new ways to mark our own birthdays as well.

*Audrey: "Celebrating my own birthday is gut-wrenching. But it gives me deep pleasure remembering the gleam in Jess's eyes as she gave me a gift. Now much of the joy I get on that day is vicarious. For instance, I take joy in bringing pleasure to my loved ones. I feel Jess's radiant smile beaming down on me."*

*Carol: "I savor the memory of my last birthday with Lisa, which was five days before she died. I save the blouse she gave me as a gift. I don't wear it. I look at it in my closet. The first couple of years, I didn't want presents, a cake, or anything."*

*Phyllis: "I can't deal with a big birthday celebration or parties in my honor. I take celebrations in small doses now."*

*Rita: "The year before Michael died, he, his brother and his father made a surprise birthday party for me. Michael was so tickled to have done this. I remember how he looked as I walked in. I miss that love from him."*

*Ariella: "My birthday is in February, as was Michael's and my father's. They're both gone now. Bob gives me a gift in Michael's name. It touches me, but still it is difficult to celebrate."*

Most of us keep the memory of our children alive in the minds of others by giving gifts in their names that are symbolic, such as butterflies or angels.

And then there are the balloons. Balloons are free, they are beautiful, they dance. Balloons romp about as if they are having fun and . . . best of all . . . they float toward heaven. Balloons are for us a means of communicating with our children. We set balloons free as a way of greeting our lost children and sending our love up to them.

It has, in fact, become the focus of our New Year's Eve celebration. Each year, we gather together along with our spouses at the home of one of our close-knit group. We write messages on the balloons and release them into the sky at the stroke of midnight. It lifts our hearts and our spirits and is a positive way of welcoming in the new year.

We negotiate our way through the holidays, birthdays and anniversaries in other ways as well. Unless forced to do so for family reasons beyond our control, we will not go to a restaurant on Mother's Day.

*Lorenza: "One time we went to a restaurant on Mother's Day, and the waitress asked if we had any mothers at our table. I told her no."*

*Barbara E.: "They hand you a flower, and you want to take that flower and tell them to stuff it."*

*Phyllis: "I go right to the cemetery with the flower they give me."*

One of us was able to again mark the Passover holiday, which she and her family had been unable to bear doing for several years, by honoring her deceased son at the seder table.

*Maddy: "Spring brings Passover, and at the Passover seder we read of the ten plagues, the worst of them being the slaying of the first-born son. Moses told the Jews in ancient Egypt to put lamb's blood on their doorposts so their homes would be passed over and their sons would be spared. Why wasn't my son spared? I skipped Passover seders for years after Neill's death. But my husband then decided to begin having seders in our home. To my surprise, it has worked out. Now we honor Neill in many ways. It is traditional to set out a glass of wine for the prophet Elijah. I set one out for Neill as well, using a glass with the logo of his beloved Rensselaer Polytechnic Institute imprinted on it. And I busy myself in the kitchen, out of earshot of the reading of passages that would upset me."*

*Audrey: "The memory of Jessie making the traditional Passover charoses in her own special way and the empty seat at the table rendered me incapable of making the seder meal for the first seven years."*

No matter the religion or the manner of observance, if it is something that simply cannot be ignored, then the way to survive it is to change the tradition.

*Barbara E.: "We don't celebrate holidays on the traditional date anymore. We get together on the day after."*

*Lorenza: "After Marc's death, we could no longer go out and buy a Christmas tree. Traditionally, we used to go out as a family and Marc would help in the selection. So we started a new tradition. We had a white pine that grew in a pot outside our home. We began bringing it in at Christmas time and decorating it with seashell ornaments that my husband made. We later gave the ornaments to friends and family in Marc's memory for their Christmas trees. And then, this year, we decided to donate the white pine tree to a children's school to help beautify their grounds."*

Ariella's son Michael was an only child. She and her husband have found the most comfortable way in which they can mark holidays is to ignore them whenever they can, an option only because they have no other children.

*Ariella: "Bob and I made decisions about dealing with holidays. We were on the same page. We agreed to cancel holidays because we could. Michael passed away in March and the first Mother's Day was horrible. On the first Father's Day, I 'asked' Michael to help me pick something for his Dad. I decided to buy him some tapes, something that played an important role in Michael's life. Michael had a boom box and I found four CDs there. I heard the song "You Gotta Be Strong." It blew me away that this was the last song he was listening to before his death. I cried more that day than ever."*

Of course when there are other children to consider, ignoring holidays is not always a realistic or feasible alternative. Oftentimes we must overcome our own emotions and dreads and give precedence to the thoughts and feelings of surviving children.

*Barbara G.: "That first Chanukah after Howie died I did not want to light candles. I could not celebrate. But my youngest son wanted to carry on the tradition. I spoke to my counselor about it. She said I must; she said that I dare not darken the holiday of lights for my son."*

*Carol: "We have two other children and five grandchildren. It was too agonizing for me to make that first seder meal after Lisa died, so we invited everyone to come to a catering place. It was painful, but not as bad as it would have been at home. Then, a few years later, my eldest grandson—he was ten at the time—objected. He wanted Thanksgiving at home. So I did it for him. Now we have the seder at home, too, and I mention Lisa. I'm glad we were able to bring the holidays home again."*

*Audrey: "The holidays held so many family traditions. They would have*

been traditions passed down to my child. Now they have lost most of their meaning. They have become so sorrowful. We've tried to make new traditions. For several years, we took the family skiing at Thanksgiving time instead of staying
home. Spending time with my daughter Deborah and my grandchildren brings
me comfort."

Barbara E.: "At holidays during that first year, we didn't mention Brian's
name out loud. Everyone thought about him, but we were all afraid to say his
name for fear we would break down. Brian has twin cousins born eighteen
months after he died. They never knew him, but they have helped our family to
talk again about Brian. They wanted to hear about 'the boy in the pictures, the
boy who had the bedroom with the closed door, the boy whose name made Aunt
Barbara cry.' I found I was able to tell them about Brian's illness and how I felt
about his death. They listened intently and I felt safe in talking with them.
Eventually, it led to my being able to talk to others as well."

While traveling in the early days of bereavement offers no relief,
with time, traveling can become a way to remove some of the pressures
and stress of dealing with family and holiday traditions.

Lorenza: "We thought to go out and look for a small town without holiday
spirit."

Vacations, of course, often remind us of vacations taken when our
children were young. As we mentioned previously, we cannot go to the
locations, sometimes not even to the state, where our children died; we
also cannot go to destinations we visited with them that hold remem-
brances of happy family times. When we travel today, we prefer to go
where we have never been before; brand-new places do not conjure up
images we cannot bear to revisit.

Maddy is greatly comforted by the Compassionate Friends conferences, be they national or regional. Consequently, she and her husband
Cliff often plan a vacation around a conference, attendance at which she
describes as a "shot in the arm."

When bereaved parents meet and discuss their own coping mea-
sures, they are able to share ideas for getting through those days we
would rather forget. Sometimes it is the smallest and most insignificant
hint that turns out to be a major boost.

*Maddy:* "Calendars became my enemies. I always looked forward to new calendars as reminders of upcoming pleasant events. Now they are a painful reminder of what once was and will be no longer. The best calendars I've had since Neill's death were sent to me by a woman in England. She too is a bereaved mother. The English calendars are great because their holidays are different from ours. There is no Memorial Day, Independence Day or Thanksgiving to mock me."

Not a holiday, not a family memory from the past, but a day that becomes forevermore etched into our very being is the anniversary of our child's death. The first anniversary is particularly brutal. And when it occurs at the time of a traditional holiday, as it does for some of us, when everyone else is celebrating, it can be particularly gut-wrenching. Lisa Barkin Gootman and Jessica Cohen were both buried as the rest of the country was celebrating the Fourth of July. Michael Long died on St. Patrick's Day.

*Ariella:* "I remember on the first anniversary of Michael's death we didn't know what we would do. And people just started coming. They came with flowers, with presents, neighbors, friends, people I didn't expect. We thanked Michael. We felt he had orchestrated the entire day."

*Barbara G.:* "The first anniversary of Howie's death fell on Yom Kippur and the cemetery was closed. We went there anyway, and although the gates were closed, we saw a slight opening. We pushed ourselves through. It was something we had learned about from other parents at a Compassionate Friends meeting."

*Phyllis:* "On the first anniversary, we held a memorial service in our home. Family and friends came. A friend led a prayer service. That's what we did . . . I didn't know what else to do."

While it is not required in the Jewish religion that an unveiling of the headstone occur on the first anniversary of a death, some families prefer to do so, and the practice has become something of a tradition. The Eisenbergs followed the tradition.

*Barbara E.:* "We decided to have a small unveiling, just the immediate family. I didn't call anybody or make it known. But I was overwhelmed when all Brian's friends showed up. I don't like to speak publicly, but I wrote something

*and spoke at the unveiling in the cemetery prior to going back to our house. A*
*portion of what I said follows:*

> *You all know how competitive Brian was. How important it was for him*
> *to win. We're finding it hard to throw out anything that belonged to him,*
> *especially things that he worked so hard to get and that meant so much to*
> *him. We would like to share these trophies, which were so dear to him, with*
> *his friends. Please think of them as a memento of a young friend who*
> *showed such inner strength and who faced everything with spirit, determi-*
> *nation and courage.*
>
> *Please try and do a mitzvot everyday—just a small good deed, and say,*
> *"This is for my friend Brian," who didn't have the opportunity to do*
> *enough of his own good deeds. Think of him often and we know he will*
> *smile down on you.*

*The unveiling was the only time our daughter went to the cemetery. At first*
*Mike and I used to go there regularly. I would go with him because I was afraid*
*to go alone. But after a year, I started going alone. It was quite emotional. I*
*would cry on my way there and talk to Brian. Now I can go and I'm not*
*afraid."*

We employ the coping mechanisms that we use on a day-to-day basis to get through death anniversaries as well. On that day, we might go
out and buy something we know our child would have enjoyed, or do
something they liked to do. We use the anniversary to remember our
children in solemn ways as well. The Collettis, for instance, started the
Marc Colletti Environmental Fund, because Marc who died in a fishing
accident, loved the water.

*Lorenza: "We have a fishing outing for underprivileged children that we*
*sponsor in early September, just before the anniversary of Marc's death. We have*
*a marine biologist on board the boat to teach the children about the ecosystem and*
*marine life, things which were so dear to Marc. The event keeps our minds fo-*
*cused, and we are comforted by the thought that we are keeping his dream alive."*

On the first anniversary of Marc's death, his widow Kate planned a beautiful and touching ceremony. Family and friends gathered by the water's edge where his coworkers had placed a plaque on a large boulder in Marc's memory. Kate read a poem and all those in attendance left a flower at the boulder. Everyone then attended a very moving church mass in Marc's memory, also planned in every detail by Kate.

At a luncheon following the mass, Kate showed a video she had commissioned depicting Marc's life from his birth to the time of his death. Lorenza recalled being surprised to see footage of her son bungee jumping, something that she had always cautioned him against doing. It brought both smiles and tears to everybody in the room.

As with all things, time softens the edges, removes the sharp pangs and gives some surcease from pain. Even the anniversary of a death no longer tears into us with the same fury.

*Phyllis:* "*In fact, on the tenth anniversary of Andrea's death, Mel and I were able to travel to the Virgin Islands to attend the wedding of a close friend's son.*"

*Rita:* "*To my disbelief ten years have passed, and with much prayer and support from family and friends, we have survived. On the tenth anniversary, several of Michael's closest friends set up a memorial service at his high school. There was a mass and one of the Catholic brothers, who had been one of Michael's closest friends in their school years, cooked lasagne for everybody. I spoke at the service. And then they traded stories of Michael all night, some I'd never heard before.*

"*Gratitude has entered my life now. I am thankful for having had Michael and always will be the mother of two wonderful sons. Our son is no longer with me physically, but he is always within me. The other son, bless him, is my tomorrow. There is a future.*"

## MICHAEL LONG

Michael was our whole world. He was our only child, a gift born to us on a cold February morning in 1975 after six frustrating, anxious years of fertility tests. Never was a baby welcomed more heartily into this world.

But, within weeks, something was terribly wrong. Michael developed flulike symptoms. The doctors found that his blood count was alarmingly low, and our precious infant had to undergo a spinal tap and a blood transfusion. He rallied at first, but within weeks he needed yet another hospitalization, another blood transfusion. The doctors told us they suspected our baby suffered from aplastic anemia, a condition in which the bone marrow does not function properly. Michael's immune system was compromised. They said the beautiful baby we had waited so long for could die. Bob and I were in shock. The doctors said Michael should undergo blood tests every few weeks.

We got lucky. Michael grew into a handsome, bright, active preschooler, and we stopped going for frequent blood tests. His annual blood counts taken during routine checkups were always low normal, but he seemed healthy. We thought we had beaten the odds.

The years flew by. Michael was an all-around kid. If it had wheels, he loved it. He had every Matchbox car ever created and as a result could name every car on the road. As an only child, he learned to amuse himself. He would spend hours lining up his tiny cars and moving them about the little village he built for them.

Our son loved sports; his travels with the soccer team as a young child became a way of life for all of us. He mastered tennis and learned to ski like a pro. In 1984, he was thrilled to go with us on a ski vacation in Austria. The image of my exquisite nine-year-old son gliding down the mountain remains engraved on my heart forever.

By the age of sixteen, Michael was 5'10" and 175 pounds. He was handsome and sporty looking with curly brown hair, a gorgeous smile and an aversion to high school. He wanted out of the classroom and found a way to double up on courses in his junior year so as to graduate a year ahead of his friends. He completed his English requirements in night school with thoughts of eventually pursuing a career in journalism.

Michael was always very comfortable around adults, probably again due to his being an only child. He loved being with us and we with him. During high school, he had chosen to work at a nursing home as a community service. It pointed to his unique capacity for combining the sweetness of youth with the wisdom of age. He was kind and compassionate and touched by the difficulties the elderly faced. We used to say that he would bring home both stray people and stray animals.

Our serenity was not meant to last. In 1991, still at age sixteen, Michael developed an extreme fatigue. More blood tests, more bad news. We were told that he was again in danger of dying and would ultimately need a bone-marrow transplant. We opted once again to wait and see what would happen.

Michael rallied, and the following summer was his best ever. He worked at a country club tennis court, he met Lauren, his first—and only—love; he had a car. The world was his.

Michael had just begun college, and he had reached a point in his life where he was confident and happy with himself. He was full of dreams and aspirations; he aspired to become a broker and earn millions of dollars. Lauren shared his dreams.

He still played his beloved sports; he enjoyed the beach, the movies, cars, pizza, travel and wristwatches. Yet when he wanted any of these things, it was important to him that he earn them for himself. He never wanted us to give him anything, preferring to work part-time jobs to pay his own way.

We considered ourselves a typical family with typical worries. We fretted over finances, Michael's education, his driving, his future. At the age of almost twenty, Michael was someone we could count on. What we never counted on was losing him.

On November 7, 1994, Michael was sick with what again appeared to be the flu. He went to the doctor and was sent immediately to the hospital for a blood transfusion. Things went from bad to worse. This time our strapping son was diagnosed with Fanconi's anemia, a rare and usually fatal blood disorder. Our typical family was facing a death sentence.

We were told that the time had come for Michael to undergo a bone-marrow transplant. He was placed on the bone-marrow registry in hopes of finding a match, and meanwhile there were transfusions, blood tests, more transfusions, more tests. Michael's veins were difficult to access, so these procedures brought him nightmares and pain.

As sick as he was, at Christmas Michael's passion for caring about everything and everyone did not forsake him. He ordered gifts for all his loved ones by using the phone at his hospital bedside and his own credit card. That was his way.

On Super Bowl Sunday, January 15, 1995, Michael was placed in the hospital's bone-marrow unit in preparation for a transplant slated for February 7, his twentieth birthday. The chemotherapy and radiation he was given to wipe out his immune system prior to the procedure made him terribly sick.

He called me one night from the hospital and shared his fears.

"Mom, they don't know what they are doing," he said. "They are going to kill me. Please take me home."

I wish I had.

Another time, I overheard him in conversation with my cousin. He never knew I heard him say, "I don't know what will happen to my parents if something happens to me."

Finally, the bone-marrow transplant was done and Michael improved for a time. We were full of hope. His blood count rose, he looked and felt better. He was trying to deal with the whole situation as best he could. I recall the mother of one of his friends referring to him as "a silent warrior."

And then on March 3, our hopes were crushed. Michael was having trouble breathing. The doctors insisted they must try to remove fluid from his lungs. Michael resisted.

That day he said no to further tests. I begged him to allow the doctors to do as they said they must. Finally, he said, "Okay, Mom, you win."

Those were the last words my beautiful son ever said to me, and I have relived the heartache of that conversation ever since.

Michael was placed on a ventilator. We saw the fear in his eyes until he was given morphine and tranquilizers. Following the procedure, our son's condition worsened, he slipped into a coma and died alone in the hospital just after midnight on March 17.

He had escaped the pain and horror of his bone-marrow transplant experience. Death was better than suffering.

I do not know the words to adequately describe the depths to which we miss Michael. He was so alive. It is still almost impossible all these years later to believe he is gone.

Ariella Long

## Seven

# Love, Laughter, and Gratitude

We originally titled this chapter Love and Laughter, but as we thought through what we wanted to say in it, we realized we had to add the word "gratitude." We are forever indebted to those who have stood by us when we needed not only someone to lean upon, but someone to pick us up when we so often stumbled and fell.

Were it not for these extraordinary people, we might never again have experienced laughter. They are, of course, first and foremost, family members.

Carol: "After Lisa died, I lost my desire to live. The constant calls from my sister, brother and my friends who cared about me helped to rekindle my spirit. They looked for books for me to read, drove me because I couldn't drive, took me out to eat, made dinner for us and did many other things. The warmth and concern from my daughters, sons-in-law and grandchildren was also very important *to me. Most of all, it was my husband, who although he loved Lisa as much as I do, still wanted to live life. He dragged me along with him even at a time when he was dealing with his own pain."*

Barbara G.: *"If I were left alone, I would likely spend my life not responding to anything. But I have two other children. When I am with my sons and their wives, and now my grandson, I am very different.*

*"This year, for the first time in many years, we did not go away for our wedding anniversary. We stayed in our new home and invited our children to be with us. It was a wonderful evening. It could have been perfect if only Howie were with us. Always things are bittersweet."*

To a great extent the extraordinary people who have restored us to love and laughter are our similarly bereaved friends. They understood precisely what it was that we were feeling and continue to feel to this day.

Ariella: *"Our life now is centered on the love, understanding and support of our Compassionate Friends. But after five years, we began to socialize with non-bereaved friends as well. Still, we are very selective. We need to be around people who are spiritual and understanding and do not demand anything of us. Life is precarious; those we socialize with must understand that."*

Sometimes the people to whom we owe a debt of gratitude are people we barely knew, or at least did not know well; people who simply stepped forward and knew instinctively how to lessen our burden.

Sometimes they were coworkers who listened attentively as we went on and on about our children, coworkers who offered us something as simple as a glass of water when we seemed parched and at our wit's end, and who sometimes gave a heartfelt hug for no reason other than they felt we needed it just then.

Audrey: *"They are the people who helped us to take baby steps when we couldn't even crawl, people like Jessica's video production teacher. He devoted an entire summer to putting together a memorial service celebrating Jess's life. He devoted almost two years to overseeing development of a memorial garden at the high school. He included Irv and I in the development process and engaged the community in fund-raising and planting. He places flowers on her grave on her* birthday. *The most beautiful thing is that he is not afraid to mention her name in front of us . . . as so many people are."*

Rita: *"I remember so well a friend who wrote to me and described in great detail the last time she had seen Michael. She wrote of his smile, what he wore. She recalled so much. It was wonderful and it made me feel wonderful."*

And so with time and a great deal of help, we have learned to laugh again . . . surely not with the degree of abandon, spontaneity and joyousness we once knew, but laugh we do on occasion, particularly when we are in each other's company.

Phyllis: *"I remember that first time we women who had met through the Compassionate Friends took our friendship to another level. It was when we traveled to a friend's condominium in Massachusetts on a winter weekend. We drove in two cars. We were so busy talking, eating our bagels and drinking our coffee that we lost the lead car and started following another car. It brought us so much laughter. And then we spoke of politics, of money, our families . . . the things that 'civilians' speak about.*

*"We rekindled feelings of hope, security and love. If you can share your feelings and stories with a friend, you will never be alone. Beyond that, there is an unspoken communication between us."*

For some of us, that was actually the very first time we truly let down our guard and enjoyed ourselves without the accompanying guilt that oftentimes affects us when we laugh in public. Outward expressions of enjoyment by the bereaved can produce some complex emotions both in ourselves and in those who see us laughing aloud . . . or so it seems, at least to us.

Rita: *"At first the newly bereaved person is offended at hearing other bereaved people laugh. But laughing is a good thing. In fact, with time we often laugh too hard. . . . It's really just like crying. We can laugh with the same pain in our laughter as we used to let out in our crying."*

Lorenza: *"The light moments in my life occur when I am in the company of other bereaved mothers. I seem to be more relaxed with them. We can talk, laugh and cry together. To an outsider it seems we are having fun. They do not realize that we never can completely let go and forget what originally drew us together."*

*Carol:* "*The first time I laughed was when there was a holiday party with other bereaved parents and we came and people were telling jokes. We laughed, and it was like crying.*"

Love never left our lives throughout our terrible ordeal. While it was oftentimes difficult to outwardly express love or to verbalize our feelings for our spouses, our surviving children and our grandchildren, love did not disappear from our lives. It was there all the while, hidden beneath our tears and behind our broken hearts, quietly waiting to show itself once we grew strong enough to allow it to emerge once again.

We bereaved feel a strange guilt because our deceased children cannot experience something pleasant that we may experience.

*Maddy:* "*When I am at a restaurant or on a trip or at the movies and I see young people, I think it should be Neill that's there, not me. So far, I haven't been able to get over that. I'm trying to get beyond it. I'm trying to set that goal for myself.*"

*Ariella:* "*Michael loved going to the movies and having pizza, going on long drives, boating. I do all those simple things that he can't do.*"

*Barbara E.:* "*Sometimes when I do something Brian would have enjoyed, I feel that I am leaving him behind. And when you do anything new, you feel very guilty about doing it and enjoying it.*"

*Lorenza:* "*Sometimes when I have a day when I seem to be absorbed in an activity, I pay a price later in guilt. How dare I have a good day when my son is dead?*"

There is often an inner voice tearing at us and telling us we oughtn't to enjoy a beautiful landscape or a new adventure because our child cannot do the same.

*Ariella:* "*When we have a beautiful sunset, I wish Michael were here to see it.*"

Each of us experiences that odd guilt. We do not know how to rid ourselves of it, but we do know its presence becomes less overwhelming with time. It doesn't go away, but it does wane somewhat. Perhaps that is only because we learn to accept it and live with it.

*Barbara E.:* "*Now when I see a beautiful sunset, I sometimes thank Brian for it.*"

What it amounts to is whatever occurs in our lives, while it may bring us some degree of happiness, is always muted, it has lost its color and its ability to make us completely forget our loss. We do not possess the same degree of passion for living that we once had.

*Phyllis: "We have two bat mitzvahs of our granddaughters coming up in our family. It won't matter to me whether or not my children invite my friends. At one time, I would have made a fuss over such an issue. Now, I won't argue. I have lost the luster to get upset over such things."*

*Audrey: "You don't have the usual everyday struggles anymore; the everyday ups and downs of motherhood that made us worry constantly about our child are gone. When your child was your whole existence, there was that constant attachment. I miss that terribly."*

*Carol: "That was what being a mother was. Worrying was my job."*

*Rita: "But I have found that the passion can return. Where I used to get depressed over an event, many times now I can say, 'Wow, think what happened today.' It's difficult for us to see ourselves changing in that way. I even have difficulty seeing it in myself, but I look at the others in our group, and I remember the way they looked when they first walked in. There is a tremendous difference."*

*Barbara E.: "But, you have to remember, sometimes that's just the effect of medication . . . if you're on medication."*

We all miss our children terribly and feel enormous gratitude that we had them for the years we did.

*Rita: "I'm thankful for Michael. I have to try to replace the negative with the positive, and now I'm able to do that."*

*Phyllis: "I would not have liked to live my life without knowing Andrea. She gave me energy; she was my mentor and her spirit kept me going. It sustained me when she was alive and now although our relationship has changed, I still feel the same way. Andrea made a difference. She was a blessing in my life and continues to be so."*

*Lorenza: "I remember there seemed to be a distinct turning point. All of a sudden, I was able to focus on the positive rather than the negative. I was able to focus on Marc's smile. At the beginning, I would only focus on Marc's struggle in the water and his death."*

*Ariella:* "*Anything you focus on grows. So, if you concentrate on the negative and the pain and suffering, you feel more of it. If you focus on what you have and what you are grateful for, that grows. At first I thought there was no future without Michael. But now I've sought a more positive approach to my life. I take care of my body, mind and soul, and the more I do, the more whole I feel and better able to deal with life. I can do things. I just take Michael along in my heart.*"

*Lorenza:* "*But you have to be ready to let that happen. It can't be rushed. We all said we wanted to die, that we couldn't go on, and truly it's not the life we had before, but it's not as bad as you think it might be. Whether we used medication or psychics, whatever, the will to survive is strong in us. Each of us has found a way.*"

Still, those of us whose children died following a lengthy illness can never erase the nagging thoughts of how they suffered. We believe it is human nature that we question why they had to endure all they did in their young lives, and we ask ourselves would it have been better for them not to have lived at all.

*Ariella:* "*Michael was very sick and suffered a great deal. During that time, we, his parents, felt there was no pain worse for us than watching him suffer. At that time, I would have given up the joy of having him for twenty years so he would not have suffered and we would not have had to watch that suffering. But in time, that has changed. I am now grateful that he was alive. I focus on the good times and the longer times when he wasn't sick.*"

*Carol:* "*I always wished when she suffered that I had never had her. Why have the child? Now, years later, I have gotten over that. The vision of all that pain fades with time. But if I had it to do over again, with the knowledge of what would happen to her, I might not have had her. I don't know. I'm confused.*"

Even those of us whose children died suddenly have wondered why they were taken so abruptly and given so little time on earth. Should we be thankful that we had them for a short time, or would it have been better not to have known them and loved them and lost them?

*Audrey:* "*There were times when the pain of losing Jess was so excruciating.*"

*But now I can think of all the pleasant times. So I am now thankful for all the joy she brought me in those too-short fifteen years."*

*Maddy: "It's our children who should have been asked that question. Neill died with hope. He did so many things, he graduated from the college of his choice, he had a girlfriend. They're the ones who should be asked if they would have wanted life if they knew it would only be for the short years they had."*

Such thoughts will probably always torment us. We try to put them out of our minds, knowing we will never have answers, at least not during life as we know it.

Meanwhile, we are maintained in the belief that our children would not want to see us carrying their deaths as a millstone around our necks. We would not want to do anything to further hurt our children.

*Barbara E.: "Brian fought death so valiantly. When he died, I wanted to die and that made me feel guilty. I contrasted my feelings with his bravery, and I felt guilt."*

*Rita: "I always feel my child can see me. I want my son to be proud of me. He was my biggest fan when he was alive. He couldn't do anything until he knew I was okay, and I couldn't do that to him now that he is gone. Do you think our children want their memory forever linked with pain?"*

*Phyllis: "It used to be that I thought of Andrea and there were tears, now I think of her and I smile, I radiate."*

*Lorenza: "And I don't want someone to say, 'Oh, that pathetic mother, all she talks about is her son.' It's not even so much what someone else will think of me, but what I think of myself. If I have several down days, I need to pick myself up. Whether it's by going for a nice walk or being with an understanding friend, I need to keep a balance in my life by finding something that makes me go on. Sometimes I go to church. It's not so much for the religion, so much as it is that it grounds me and makes me look at what's important in life and where I want to go in my life."*

But none of us was able to think in such rational terms early on. As we've said before, the time when grief begins to lessen it's hold on us cannot be rushed, and it follows no timetable. For some, it is sooner rather than later. There is no way of telling when it will begin to lift, but begin it will. At some point, we were able to stop thinking of our child's death all day, every day.

Barbara E.: *"I remember one morning about nine months after Brian died when I woke up and he was not the first thing I thought about. I looked out the window to see what the weather was like, and then I was so shocked that Brian was not my first thought. I caught myself and asked myself, 'What do you care about the weather?'"*

Phyllis: *"That happened to me at about nine months as well."*

Maddy: *"And it's not the same with husbands and wives. Sometimes when I might not be thinking of Neill, Cliff remembers, as if by radar. We bought some furniture about three years after Neill died. I was relieved as we left the store; I wasn't even thinking about Neill. But as soon as we got into the car, Cliff started to cry. He was upset that Neill would never see the new furniture, never sit on the new couch. It's as if when I'm off of it, Cliff is on it."*

Barbara G.: *"Our husbands have grown, too. Last year, Bruce was playing golf and he got a hole in one. He was ecstatic, but then he got teary-eyed because he couldn't tell Howie about it. Still he was able to verbalize that to me and tell me how he felt. He too has grown and changed, of course."*

If at all possible, we go out of our way to avoid those triggers that bring back the tragedy. Or we learn to deal with them as best we can.

Rita: *"You can desensitize yourself over a period of time. Michael died in a car. Over time, I had to get back into a car again. I could not possibly never again get into a car."*

Lorenza: *"Marc died on the water's edge and I find it hard to go to that beach. When it rains a lot in summer, I feel better, no one goes to the beach. I can't sit by the beach and watch the waves on a sunny day. But, when it's a nice, rainy, cloudy day, then I can sit by the water. I have a photo of my son sitting there watching the water and that's what I do. I can feel some serenity that way."*

Barbara E.: *"Mike and I still live in the same community in which Brian grew up. We pass the same soccer fields and parks in which he played since he was five years old and the same elementary and high school that Brian attended. The memories are mostly good now, and many times it brings Brian closer to us."*

Some of us like to say our deceased children continue to offer us "gifts." Others of us take offense at that word. Ariella in particular is able to think that events that occur now in her life are "gifts" from Michael. Readers will likely agree or disagree. That is the way it is with bereavement. . . . There is no set path, there is always deviation and there are great differences, but eventually all seem to lead to a form of acknowledgment and, eventually, yes, even laughter.

*Ariella: "Our kids now offer us gifts. I'm grateful for the feeling that I have at all times that Michael is watching over us. I think that he is creating opportunities for us. Things happen, opportunities crop up that are rare and we were not looking for them. Wonderful things happen, as if a flower is growing from cement.*

*"For instance, Bob and I now live on a boat. Bob and Michael always wanted to do that; I was hesitant. I was afraid of the weather. What would I do with all my stuff? What kind of community would I have? But they wanted it badly. Then, when Michael passed, we had to make a decision. I swear to you that it was Michael's words in my head that said, 'Go for it.' "*

Naturally, there is room for disagreement among us, as there should be.

*Phyllis: "I resent the word 'gift.' I understand what Ariella is saying, and I am grateful for the family that I have. But to say that Andrea left me a gift? I don't like that word."*

*Lorenza: "Of course we would trade all the gifts in the world to have our children back in our arms."*

There are times when we do seem to receive guidance from our deceased children. We seem to think in terms that they would use, and we wonder if those words are coming from them. Whatever it is, it helps to make our lives easier so that we do smile and laugh again, particularly if we can think that they are with us somehow and watching over us, wanting us to find enjoyment here on earth. We talk to them and we feel better knowing they have that place—forever—in our lives.

*Barbara G.: "My visits to the cemetery are the perfect example of the healing powers of time. At first I cried bitterly, I was angry. I stamped my foot at the gravesite, ranting and raving that Howie did not belong there. When his brothers married, I buried a copy of each invitation for him to have, when his nephew was born, I brought him a birth announcement. I always have silent conversations with Howie and bring him up to date on family doings. I ask him to look after his brothers.*

"*And then, not long ago, I was bent over the grave having my one-sided conversation when I realized I was joking with him and speaking to him just as I did when he was alive. This was a first for me and I was glad when I realized I was doing it.*"

Of course, there are still many times when we feel down, and we stop and ask ourselves if we really are healing or if we are just becoming better actresses. No, we agree . . . we all are truly recovering.

*Ariella: "I'm grateful for who I am today. I like the new me and I like that we celebrate our kids' lives and not their deaths."*

*Rita: "I could not dance for years. Michael loved to dance; now when I dance I am sure my son smiles. Now when I dance, I am celebrating his life and all the beauty and love he brought to mine."*

## NEILL S. PERRI

I married my first husband, John Perri, when I was eighteen years old and he was twenty. People speculated that we "had to get married," but that wasn't true. We waited three years to get pregnant. Our first child was carefully planned and very much wanted. We had a son, and we named him Neill.

He had brown curly hair and big brown eyes with long lashes. Most of my friends weren't married when he was born, and they doted on him. Neill was the first grandchild of John's and my parents, the first nephew of our siblings, and the first great-grandchild of both sets of my grandparents. My maternal grandparents were still young enough to babysit for him, play with him and cherish him. Sadly, they were still alive to bury him.

When Neill was four years old, John and I had a second son whom we named Phillip. So began the closest and purest relationship between two brothers that I ever witnessed. We used to joke that they were twins born four years apart. Neill was shy with other children, and Phillip became his best friend.

The statistics are against teenage marriages, and mine was no different. Immaturity on both our parts was probably the real reason for my divorce. Phillip was still a baby, but Neill was devastated. He never got over the dissolution of what to him was the perfect family. Although he acted out at home and took out his rage on John, me and, later, his stepfather Cliff, his scholastic record was impeccable.

Teachers loved and praised Neill. In fifth grade, he became a school crossing monitor and, by sixth grade, he was the lieutenant of the squad. He won many awards, commendations and medals throughout secular and Hebrew school and was accepted into the college of his choice, Rensselaer Polytechic Institute. In his late teens and early adulthood, Neill fought and won his hardest battle. He overcame his shyness, made good friends, began dating and came into his own as a young man. Although he earned a master's degree in engineering from RPI, he chose to work in retail for a drug store chain.

Neill's career advanced rapidly. He was set to begin a managerial position shortly after his summer vacation. During that vacation, he attended his cousin's bat mitzvah with John's side of the family, went to Connecticut on an overnight trip with Cliff and me, and spent time with Phillip. On Wednesday, June 14, he went to a large amusement park with his friends, including the girl I hoped might have become his wife. On the morning of Thursday, June 15, he took a bus trip to Atlantic City with my mother.

As I was getting ready for work that day, I received a telephone call from my aunt. She summoned me to her home, and Phillip went with me. We arrived to find my aunt and uncle frozen in place, the color drained from their faces. Wordlessly, my aunt handed me the phone. My brother Richard was on the line.

"There is no easy way to tell you this," he said. "Maddy, Neill died." At that moment, the worst in my life, heaven and earth and hell became one. The second worst moment came as I turned to Phillip and told him that his brother was dead. He crumpled in my arms, sobbing.

My mother was in anguish when I spoke with her on the phone. She had first called my aunt with the tragic news because she could not bear to tell me herself. She related that she and Neill had both taken naps on the bus. She awakened to find him in a sound sleep and noticed that his arm had turned blue. On their arrival in Atlantic City, she said to the casino representative who met them, "There's something wrong with my grandson." The woman took one look at Neill and cleared the bus. Paramedics were brought on board, but my beautiful son was already dead. His body was removed to a nearby hospital, while my mother was taken to a room in the casino hotel by a security guard who stayed with her.

My husband Cliff, my former husband John, his wife Mary, my brother Richard, Phillip and I met my mother in Atlantic City. When we were told there had to be an autopsy, we found a local rabbi to sanction it. As it turned out, the rabbi had lost a child. I phoned my best friend Jill and told her Neill had died. She didn't believe me. She thought to herself, "Well, Maddy has finally cracked up." To this day, we both wish that had been the truth . . . that I had lost my mind rather than that Neill had died.

Everything about his death remains surreal. . . . his original death certificate listed the cause of death as "pending." Even after the autopsy, followed by a review of the slides in Trenton, New Jersey, the final death certificate listed the cause of death as "undetermined." After much pleading, I finally was sent a letter that stated he died from a "probable viral infection affecting the heart."

When we saw Neill in the morgue, he lay on a bed, covered up to his face with a blanket. He was translucent, the blue veins showing through his skin. But he looked so peaceful. There was no fear or pain in his face. From across the room, I whispered what I had said to him at bedtime throughout his life. "Good night Neill. I love you. No dreams."

Cliff wrote a poem, "Gentle Guardian," to read at Neill's funeral. It described Neill's honesty, intelligence and unique style, his anguish over his parents' divorce and the bright future he had created for himself. The poem concluded by asking, "Why did God take him with so much to miss? Without sirens or shrieks or alarms? God took him so gently with just a kiss, he died in his Grandma's arms. Before you feel anger or cry with rage, or just don't know what you should feel, there's a new Guardian Angel reporting today. 'Hello, my name is Neill.'"

Neill was spiritual. He believed in God, heaven and destiny, and I loved him with all my being. At age sixteen, he wrote an autobiographical essay for school. It finished by saying, "I have a few basic goals for the future. I want to drive a car soon. I want to go to college . . . I am probably going to major in electronics engineering. My main goal is to have a long, happy life."

By June 15, 1995, Neill had completed two of his three goals.

Madelaine Perri Kasden

*Eight*

# Until We Meet Again

Will we ever again see our children? Where, when, how? What will they look like? Will we ever be able to speak with them and hold them close? This is the chapter that offers no definitive answers.

When our sons and daughters were torn from us, we were left with gaping wounds that cannot heal unless and until we can once again reach out and touch them and know that they are well. What wouldn't we give to once again see them smile? See them as they are today?

We all expected to see our children grow older. There would be grandchildren who resembled them, who resembled us. We would see our own children take on the responsibilities and the cares and woes that come with adulthood and eventual middle age. We were robbed of those joys of passage.

*Ariella: "It bothers me that someday I'll be old and have no one to leave things to. There's no continuation. There's no one to worry about, or care about. It's going to end with Bob and me and that's a very sad thing. I try not to dwell on it too much."*

We have even been robbed of the mixed emotions parents experience upon seeing their children lose their youthful good looks and become balding, aging adults.

*Lorenza: "It bothers me that I don't know what my son would look like at forty. When his friends come to the door and they haven't changed, I am glad because that means he'd still look the same, too. But five years from now, it's going to be so painful because his friends will change. Marc is always going to be a young man. I'll never know what he would have looked like."*

*Audrey: "Jessica was not even sixteen when she died. Now all her friends are grown and starting their careers. Where would Jessie be?"*

*Ariella: "I decided to stop seeing Michael's friends. This way I can keep him and them in my mind the way they were. I prefer that."*

*Barbara E.: "Recently at a restaurant, my husband and I saw an elementary school friend of Brian's seated at the first table with his parents. So many thoughts and feelings passed over us at once. We spoke with them and learned that the young man is now an investment banker and his sister had graduated from law school. Meanwhile, in our hearts and dreams, Brian is still a twenty-one-year-old fun-loving college student. Although it's been years since he lost his battle with leukemia that is how we still experience him.*

*"When I was confronted with the reality of this young man and his fortunate family, I felt jealous. Confusion after all these years. How am I supposed to feel? The guilt crept in. I didn't want that family to think that I'm over it. I'm not and never will be. Confusion. I can either rage against my feelings or accept them. It's a constant battle."*

With the advent of modern computer technology, graphic artists are now able to project what a person might look like years into the future. The procedure is now commonly done in police investigations to aid in the search for kidnapped children who will have aged since the time of their disappearance. We have toyed with the idea of taking our children's photos to a computer artist in an effort to see what they might have looked like with the passage of time. None of us has done it so far, but it is extremely tempting.

As a group, we are relatively united in our thinking when it comes to handling those heart-wrenching times that keep recurring, such as the awkward silence that still comes during a conversation with an old friend, the holiday that is wrought with memories of happier days, or the soothing of a husband whose grieving is out of sync with our own. These are tangible dilemmas, and while they may be difficult and sometimes even impossible to resolve, there is at least a way of making them more tolerable. . . . There is something of an answer.

Whether or not we will ever again meet our children is a question fraught with mystery, anxiety and complexity. Until that day in the future when we ourselves leave this earth, all we can offer are our own imaginations, prayers and desires, and of course our dreams.

*Ariella: "I always picture Michael as being our guide, watching and protecting us."*

*Maddy: "I feel that Neill is the wiser one now."*

*Phyllis: "In my dreams, Andrea says to me that she has a life. I feel that if she were here today—and if she was, she would be a woman in her late thirties—she would not want me butting into her life. I have that dream repeatedly and it gives me comfort. Last September, on her birthday, I dreamed about her. In my dream, I said to her, 'You know, Andrea, it's enough.' She said, 'Get a life.' "*

*Rita: "Like Michael would say, 'Chill out, Ma.' "*

It is impossible for us to speak with one voice about whether or not we will see our children again. Our thoughts on the subject draw deeply upon our own psyches, beliefs and dreams. In truth, we do not even understand our own feelings on the subject.

*Lorenza: "Going to church has always been part of my culture and tradition. I was what one would call a good Catholic. I attended Mass regularly and was familiar with all the prayers. Now, I realize that in saying some of the prayers, I was not aware of the significance of every word, I just said them. My faith had never been put to a test, so I thought I believed in God.*

*"After my son's death, I became aware of the significance of every word in every prayer. It is painful to hear that Jesus raised Lazarus from the dead. What of my son? It is difficult to hear that the apostles were told to walk on water and nothing would happen to them. Marc drowned. Do I believe in the resurrection of the dead? Where will all the bodies go?*

*"And so my religion has been shaken. I go to mass now and I find some comfort there because it is calming to have hope, to dream and to look forward to a happy ending one day. I pray that God gives me the gift of faith so that I can be at peace with myself.*

*"But do I believe that my son and I will meet one day? I truly don't. Would I like to believe it? I pray that one day we will meet again."*

Of our group, only Rita and Ariella can say with assuredness that they definitely believe in an afterlife and that they will one day be reunited with their sons. The rest of us either would like to believe it, but we aren't certain or we do not believe.

To speak openly and frankly of an afterlife is not something that is always acceptable to friends and acquaintances. Rita, who is a devout Catholic, confines herself to writing about it and discussing it with other bereaved parents, and refrains from talking about it in any depth with the "civilian" world. When she is with outsiders, she says only that she believes in an afterlife and that it gives her great comfort to know her son is well and that she will see him again someday. Here, however, she speaks her mind.

*Rita: "When I was young and my father died, I always felt him spiritually, that he was with me. That he existed. Believing is a gift. But for years after my son died, I wouldn't allow myself to think of being reunited with him because it would be ecstasy, too huge to deal with. I didn't want to go there because I could not deal with it emotionally. Now I envision the moment in my mind's eye.*

*"Oh, Michael, my Michael, where have you been? Are you all right? I've dreamed of this moment millions of times in my mind. Just hold me close and tell me you're fine. Please tell me the nightmare is ended, that you're real and it's not just pretend. Oh, Michael, my Michael, is this what ecstasy is? I've dreamed of this moment day in and day out. Did my dad come to greet you and escort*

*you to heaven? Were you in pain as you passed on that night? Did you miss us,*
*too, as we so ached for you? Did you dance with the angels? Was God in clear*
*sight? Oh, don't say a word. Just hold me tight."*

Ariella: *"My belief that there is an afterlife has helped me cope with the loss*
*of Michael. I am convinced that I will see him again and that he exists on a*
*higher level and is around me at all times. I've connected with Michael through*
*writing twice. I wrote down a question for which I was seeking an answer and the*
*answer came into my head. It gave me another perspective on his existence. I feel*
*that he is fine and always with me."*

The rest of us remain conflicted and confused. Will we see our children again, will we not? Is the possibility something we have created
within our own imaginations? Holding fast to the possibility that one
day we will be with our children is many times all that keeps us going
when there is a day or a night in which all else fails to grant us peace of
mind. Even if such a thought is nothing more than a delusion, we want
desperately to grasp on to it and believe it. In some ways, we are even
afraid not to believe, because as Rita has said, "They have our children."

Maddy: *"I have to believe that there's an afterlife, that someday Neill and I*
*will be reunited. Otherwise, this life makes no sense at all. When I imagine a re-*
*union with Neill, I see him in my mind's eye the way he looked at the age of*
*twenty-three when he died. He was tall, thin and had a moustache. I don't nec-*
*essarily see him smiling. I imagine him annoyed with me for the way I've been*
*living, or should I say not really living since his death. I hear him asking me why*
*if I considered his life to be so precious, I wasted so much of my own life grieving*
*for him."*

Barbara G.: *"I am no longer a religious person, nor does my religion em-*
*phasize an afterlife. However, I always picture our being reunited. Without this*
*one belief, I don't think I could have continued on after he died."*

Even those of us who acknowledge deep down that our longing to
someday meet again with our children is more fantasy than reality still
hesitate to even bring up the subject to the general public and even in
some cases to our spouses.

Audrey: *"I have said it to friends and the topic is usually dropped after I talk about it. It depends on how spiritual they are. Most people just kind of smile at you and change the subject."*

For the most part we believe that energy cannot be destroyed, we prefer to go with the school of thought that believes that it changes form. And so we continue to cherish the hope that our children exist in whatever that form may be . . . someplace. They cannot just be gone. Their souls at least must continue to exist . . . someplace.

*Lorenza: "As mothers, all of us obviously share a universal feeling that if we had a chance to meet our children, we would embrace them and be happy. It's a fantasy, but a universal one."*

*Ariella: "It's very important that we hold on to the belief that energy cannot be destroyed, that it only changes form. We read everything we can about NDE—near-death experiences—looking for clues. Everything that we say about this subject is based on the fifty-fifty chance that an afterlife could be."*

*Barbara G.: "To reinforce my conviction about an afterlife, I started reading all I could regarding near-death experiences as well as visiting psychics. It helped so much to feel that there would be a time when we would be together again."*

*Maddy: "I do believe in an afterlife. If heaven exists, I think it exists beyond human comprehension. For example, there would be no restaurants, no jewelry, no jobs there. I believe it would be much more elevated and on a level we can't imagine. It's soul, and we can't understand it"*

*Audrey: "I have mixed feelings. I want to believe."*

Even as we wait, we sense the company of our children here on earth. We talk to them, we ask for their opinions, we reach out for them. Of course, they are never there.

*Phyllis: "I love feeling that Andrea and I will meet again, but will it happen? I don't know. I don't believe in an afterlife. I want to. I would love it. Whatever will happen, I can't tell. Now, here today I can feel her touching me. I can touch her and talk to her. But when I think of her, I don't think of her as a person. I see her as like a soul, a ghost."*

*Audrey: "A lot of times I feel Jess's presence, and other times I don't know."*

*Ariella: "Having lost my only child, I struggled with the thought of 'am I still a mother?' I missed not being called Mom. But I know in my heart that I was and always will be Michael's mom. I like to think that my relationship with Michael has not ended, but rather it has changed. It is now more personal and spiritual. But it is always there."*

Carol has studied the art of meditation and uses it to good advantage. She is also capable of being hypnotized. She recalls as a child being placed under hypnosis during dental work. The rest of us have had no experience with either meditation or hypnosis. Carol believes it is because she is able to concentrate so fully and wants so much to be able to communicate with Lisa in this way that she is able to do so.

*Carol: "I use mind control. I bring myself down to a meditative state and every time I meditate I meet with Lisa. We kiss and hug and take a walk and sit together and that's it. I can go back there any time I want. I always see her at about the age of seventeen or eighteen, before she got sick. And it's a great thing. It brings a certain inner peace. When Lisa died, I could not meditate for a long time because I was mad at the meditation and at God. But then I got it back again."*

*Ariella: "It sounds wonderful. We should get someone to show us all how to do it."*

Until this writing, Carol's husband Don knew that she practiced meditation, but she had never told him that she uses it as a means of communicating with Lisa.

*Carol: "He doesn't believe in it."*

Among us, Barbara Eisenberg is the only one who cannot envision meeting her son again someday.

*Barbara E.: "I want to believe there is an afterlife and that I will meet Brian again, but deep down inside me I don't believe it's going to be. I think when I was growing up, I had more of a belief in an afterlife and being reunited with people and heaven and hell, but it all stopped when Brian died. I really never had a lot of religious faith. And I really don't see how it would work. If Brian is now a soul, how do I recognize a soul? As for prayer, people say they prayed hard and a miracle happened. We prayed. Why not us? Why didn't Brian get well?"*

Whether it be reality or fantasy, we all spend a good deal of time imagining what we will say to our children and what we will do should we ever meet them again. We write poems about it and dream about it. It is a form of escape from the reality that they are gone.

We intend to ask our children if they had any premonitions that their lives were about to end. Obviously, when tragedy strikes it is not unusual for a person to look back and wonder if there were forewarnings of what was to come. We hear such musings all the time at bereavement meetings. Among ourselves we look back and recall events that might have foretold of tragedy. One of us, for instance, lost the little boy charm from her bracelet, which held a charm for each child. That occurred just prior to the diagnosis of her son's illness.

There are always things that can be construed as signs or omens, but in our cases they proved to be all too true. Did our children know what was coming? We will ask when we see them.

*Audrey: "I think maybe Jess had a premonition about dying. One day out of the blue she commented to me, 'Do you realize one of us will have to bury the other?' I responded that I expected to be around a long time to bother her.*

*"And after Jess died, I was convinced that I was privy to information that no one else knew. I envisioned a cataclysm of such magnitude that the world would end . . . chemical warfare, an epidemic caused by a new viral strain. And then 9/11 occurred. I was right . . . she was spared."*

*Ariella: "During one of the many times Michael was in the hospital, he had two nightmares. In one he thought he was in a concentration camp and that all the people there died. In the second nightmare, he was in a sinking boat encircled by sharks. His father tried to get a lifeboat into the water to save him, but it was too late. I knew he thought he was going to die and he was terrified."*

We agonize over what our children experienced at the time of their deaths. We want to know if they experienced pain, if they knew they were dying. So many questions. Will we ever have answers?

*Phyllis: "When we meet, Andrea and I will hug and laugh about who hugs top and who hugs bottom. We'll cry, we'll smile and laugh. How much we both have missed each other. Where will we begin? Who will talk first? I'll say, 'I'm the mother, me first.' Or we'll decide to take turns. I'll ask how she got to where she is. How did she feel when she was hit by the car? What did she see and could she remember? I will tell her about my life, her father, her sister and brother's lives, her nieces and nephews, bring her up to date on her friends. (I hope I will remember.) I will want to hear what Andrea does every day. We will be so ex-*

*cited. Both our worlds at this time will be one. No more yearning, longing, empti-ness. I'll be with Andrea in Andrea's world.*

"*As her mother, I showed Andrea the way in life; now she will show me the way. I'll meet her new friends. I'll ask to see Grandma and Grandpa. Andrea will be my leader. In life, Andrea taught me how to cope and deal with people, now in death her message will be the same.*

"*I will not have any more pain. I will be free. I'll hear her famous one-liners. We'll talk about the different worlds we lived in. I'm starting my list of things we will talk about after we love each other up and touch. Now we will be together forever. I know she will recognize me because my love for her will reach her. Even if she is in a large crowd, she will feel my love for her.*

"*Eventually we will argue and I'll hear, 'Oh, Ma!' I know then I will be safe.*"

Audrey: "*When we meet again I will be too emotional to speak anything but your name Jessie, Jess, Jessica. I will hug you to me and when I gain my com-posure we will talk and you will know what has been in my heart for all these years since your death. I will continue to hold your hand for fear that you will slip away from me and you will lead me down a path of my choosing. I will choose the one in which I witness you maturing into adulthood. You will go through your last two years of high school, the anxiety of applying for colleges, waiting for your college acceptance. I will see you at your senior prom and at graduation. Next we will settle you in college and witness the tribulations of your freshman year. Would you be happy with your choice of colleges? Would you be homesick? Will you be happy with your new friends and your career choice? When I can experience the anxiety of these struggles, I will know I am in heaven.*"

Maddy: "*In the movie* Field of Dreams *Kevin Costner is asked over and over again by the spirits of the deceased ball players, 'Is this Heaven?' He re-sponds, 'No, it's Iowa.' Neill used to love Cliff's imitation of Costner saying that. When I meet with Neill I will ask, 'Is this Iowa?' and he will say, 'No, it's Heaven.'*"

Carol: "*There is nothing I want more than to hold Lisa again in my arms, to hug and kiss her and hear her sweet voice again. I don't think I will have to fill her in. I think she will know it all. Even though I have been resistant in many ways, I feel her presence at times, so she must be near me and she must know all about my life since she left this earth. I want to know where she has been and what it has been like."*

Barbara G.: *"Howie will take my hand and lead me to this new place after a hug which I can feel as I write about it; my arms wrapped around his thin body, his head towering over mine. I will show utmost restraint in not wanting to know immediately what happened to him. It will no longer matter. I would like to sit quietly alone with him and drink him in, listen to his voice, touch his hand, kiss his face, see the sparkle in his eyes and generally catch up with his life. All of my senses will then be satisfied; all that I have missed doing since 1991, I will now be able to do.*

*"I want to know what he has been doing in Heaven. Has he realized his dream of becoming an attorney and eventually a judge? Has he met the love of his life? Does he have children? Is he doing what he wanted to do, which was to just help people in need? I picture my son unfettered by life's problems, free in the glories of the heavens to pursue whatever he wishes.*

*"I know that when I take my last breath it will be with a smile on my face, for I will be going on a long journey to be reunited with a part of myself that I have missed for so long. Balanced against leaving those I love behind will be all the years when we were cheated of being with one another.*

*"I have left instructions to be buried in the dress I wore to Howie's bar mitzvah, for that holds special significance for me. Intellectually, I know that only our spirits will meet and no other baggage will go with me; but emotionally I need this special dress, so I'll be sure he'll know me when we meet in Heaven."*

As we wait, we dream. No matter the passage of time, dreams have the power to bring our children back to life. Of course, waking and finding our children are not there can just as easily plunge us into gloom.

Lorenza: *"I had a dream of Marc one night and I woke up shaking. I felt his warmth so vividly. I held my arm for the longest time. I thanked my son for the hug. It kept me happy the whole day. But one night, Joe woke up and he was crying badly. He said he had just been with Marc."*

Ariella: *"My husband said seeing Michael in his dreams was awful because he would wake up over and over and realize Michael was not there. He has a lot of dreams of Michael in which he will see him at a train station. He'll try to talk with him and Michael will be gone. He tries not to talk to Michael now in his dreams, so Michael will not go away. Then he wakes up and is depressed the whole day."*

Guilt, most of it totally groundless, is something we have lived with in varying degrees since the deaths of our children. A mother and child reunion would give us opportunity to assuage some of that guilt. As we've said, we initially thought perhaps our children were taken from us because of something we had done. Their deaths were our punishment.

Some of us still harbor a degree of that guilt years later. It may express itself in different and unusual ways, as in Barbara Eisenberg's case. She is the only one of us who, if she were to see Brian in heaven, which she doubts could occur, would hope to be able to make some changes in their relationship. Brian, was the younger of two children, and his older sister was born with physical disabilities, which always demanded the greater share of Barbara's focus.

*Barbara E.: "Brian had a tough time in our house. He had to do things to get my attention because I spent so much time with his sister. I always felt I would have time someday to make it up to him. I didn't. And I haven't really dealt with my feelings about that. I put them away. Talking here about this is making me take out my feelings and look at them. I don't like that. It's easier to just forget everything."*

If we were to see our children again, we would want them to know how we regret ever making their short lives difficult or even troublesome. We wish we could take back all the times we spanked them or refused to buy them a much-wanted toy. If we could, we would undo all the arguments we ever had with them.

If their death was sudden or accidental, we want to tell them that we continue to harbor terrible remorse that we weren't with them to comfort them as they went through their ordeal. If a child died on the water, we want them to know we still blame ourselves for teaching them to love the sea. We rue the day we bought them cars or water skis.

*Carol:* "*No matter how they died, you think there was something you could have done differently. And you blame yourself for that. You think back to all the times you yelled at them or made them do something they were mad at you for. You feel like a monster. I go back over when I was pregnant. Maybe I did something wrong. You cannot believe the soul searching I go through. Why did I make her walk home from the orthodontist?*"

*Rita:* "*If I knew my son was going to die at twenty, do you think I'd have made him go to school? Go out and earn money? If I had known, he could have had anything he wanted. But we did not raise our children to die, we raised them to live. We built such character into our son. But we didn't get a chance to finish the job. So, now we take it out on ourselves. Even if you were a perfect parent, you still feel guilt.*"

We lament and we re-examine. We go over everything we did in our lives. It's not rational to blame ourselves for the deaths of our children, but we continue to do so, even beyond those early days when blaming ourselves occupied so much of our days and nights. We want to be able to tell them face to face of our guilt. We want to hold them and tell them of our sorrow, tell them that they left this life too soon and that, could we have done so, we would have given anything to have prevented their deaths.

We want to tell them that even in death they have had a deep and lasting impact on those they touched. In dying, they have become bigger than life to those who knew them well. Their friends keep them alive in their memories, picturing them always as they were when they died, forever sixteen or twenty or twenty-five. Just as they are always within us, so they are within others who knew and loved them.

*Lorenza:* "*We sometimes wonder if our children are together. Why did this group get together? Is there a connection someplace? We all wonder about that.*"

With this book, which none of us could have written in the earlier days of our grief, we are making certain our children are not forgotten. We are ensuring that their lives made a difference. Helping another bereaved parent along the way is our tribute to them.

## MICHAEL VOLPE

Michael was always in motion. At the age of three he could swim; at four he rode a two-wheeler, and at eight he learned to water ski. At twelve he broke his foot playing tag but was back on his bike in two days, grinning from ear to ear, with the cast balanced on the pedal. Nothing could stop Michael Motion.

Some people spend their lives reacting to others. Michael was the one to watch, action personified. He was filled with a fire that burned with a fury and it compelled him to leap at and absorb anything he felt passionate about, whether it was a sport, a job or his social life. He gave no mind to schedules. Rather he welcomed each day as a new and exciting challenge to be reckoned with and conquered.

To watch Michael was to watch an athlete. He took great pains to develop an agile and well-coordinated body. The autopsy after his accident was a testament to his efforts. His body was perfect . . . perfect.

In high school, Michael ran track and was a sprinter. I know now how appropriate that was. His life would run but a short distance, but he would sprint through with enormous fervor, as if he knew the track that stretched before him would not be a long one.

Michael loved any game with a ball. He played basketball, baseball, stickball, football. The punch ball bounced off the wall in his bedroom while he was "doing homework." The football skipped down the street as he did his touchdown dance; the basketball bounced up the block as he returned from school. Even now, when I hear those sounds it breaks my heart.

He was never much for studying. You'd tell him to study in his room and then you'd hear him banging around in there, making something, improvising on a new type of pen or whatever. He went to Archbishop Molloy High School and then on to St. John's University. Still, he didn't study. He didn't have to. He was in the honors program, and he was just naturally intelligent.

Michael loved the water and we always said maybe that came from his being a Pisces. Someone once told me that fish never stopped moving. That was Michael. He loved music and he loved to dance. He knew he was a good dancer and he wasn't shy about it. He enjoyed an audience. Whenever certain songs would play he would run and get me to join him. I loved every minute of that. To this day, whenever I hear one of those songs, my heart dances again with him.

Michael adored animals and his room was home to quite a variety. He would change the salamander's toys with the frequency of a nervous parent and prod the nocturnal hamster awake during the day to enjoy its company. I even remember him once trying to pet the fish when he was moving it from one tank to another.

Faith was a mainstay in Michael's young life. He was a very spiritual person, but it was low-key. It was Michael's interest in the church that brought us back to going to mass as a family. He worked at church as a sacristan, setting up the altar. When he'd see family members, he's come down and greet them. He was a pure spirit, always bringing family together . . . all heart.

He hadn't decided what he wanted to do in life yet, possibly law, possibly veterinary medicine. But he'd only finished two years of college. That summer of 1987, he planned to return home to work with kids as a day camp counselor. He'd done that before and really enjoyed it.

Two days before Michael's death, we all attended a family wedding. I was standing inside a glass-enclosed room and looked out to see my two sons, Michael, twenty and Tommy, eighteen, arriving together. I was filled with pride as they walked in dressed to the nines . . . so beautiful, so wonderful, so gifted. They looked like movie stars. All eyes focused on them as they entered and lit up the room. I said to myself, "I am so blessed."

Michael's eyes sparkled as he looked my way, nodded his head and smiled with a sort of shy acknowledgment. The day, the scene is etched in my mind forever.

And then on a sunny Tuesday, at the very start of the summer vacation, everything changed. Michael had worked nonstop all that day filling in for a friend who had a job at a neighborhood moving company. He stopped at the gym on his way home. After dinner he took a shower and gave himself a complete overhaul . . . hair, nails, toenails, the works.

He did mention he'd vomited up his dinner, but he seemed relaxed and in a light mood. He watched a little television and left to meet a friend. He was going out locally; he would see us later.

He left through the back door, completely preened, a picture of health and beauty, not even a cavity in his mouth. I didn't get a chance to kiss him good-bye. I didn't get a chance to say, "Be careful." That was a ritual. Why was it missing that night? If I'd had the chance to say it, would it have made a difference?

My husband Tom and I went to a movie, came home and went to sleep. Our sons would always knock on our door when they arrived home. We needed to know they were safe.

At 1 A.M. I awakened startled and nervous. Why wasn't he home? Oh, well, not a big deal. I fell back to sleep.

At 4 A.M. there was a knock at the door. Our son Tommy answered. Two female police officers. They wanted to talk to us. There had been an accident at 1 A.M. Michael's car hit a pole at the Main Street exit of the Long Island Expressway.

Don't utter those words. It cannot be. . . . It cannot be.

Such a few words and my son . . . gone forever.

He was almost home. He could have walked those few blocks. Either he was cut off or the car malfunctioned, or maybe he fell asleep; we remembered he had vomited earlier in the evening. We will never know the answers. All we know is that the car swerved off the road and mounted the guard rail, rendering the brakes useless, and leading Michael on a death trip to the pole. It became a monorail of death beyond his control. For years I could not remember the word "guard rail."

Michael owned a small sports car, which worried us. That night he was driving our huge family station wagon; we called it "the tank." We kept it because our younger son was a new driver and we figured it would keep him safe. We thought we could control our sons' safety. We kept them close, we were strict parents; we thought we had the power to protect them. Michael had done dangerous things in his life. That night was not one of those times.

My son, my husband and I were emptied, shattered. We sat on the sofa huddled together, a heap of flesh. We were dead, too.

We waited for the sun to rise only to curse it. Michael had to be identified at the morgue.

"Please, God, make it be someone else. This is all a mistake. Michael will come back to us. It cannot be that he no longer walks this earth."

The one comforting thought is that my brother, Michael's uncle, was standing at the roadside praying for the victim of that accident. He had no idea it was Michael. He was traveling on the expressway and had come upon the accident scene. He stopped and prayed over the terrible wreckage. Later, he would write a beautiful poem converting the horror to a spiritual level.

The thought that I was not there will forever haunt me. I brought Michael into this world, I comforted him in sickness, attended to his wounds and broken bones. He had always wanted his mom there for re-assurance and I had always been there. This was his last wound and I wasn't there.

As we look back, we realize that Michael entwined himself with family in the days leading up to his death. He went to the beach with his dad, he visited me at the school where I taught. He looked out the window of my classroom and noticed a beautiful tree in the courtyard. He said it looked "depressed." He visited his grandmother and installed blocks in her driveway. Those blocks are now a memorial, which she will not remove. At that family wedding two days earlier, he stayed late and talked to everyone at length. He left indelible marks on everybody that week. Did he know?

At Michael's funeral, his brother Tommy eulogized him. "He taught me how to love," Tommy said.

Rita Volpe

*Nine*

# The Fathers Speak

Our sorrow runs as deep, our anguish is as all encompassing, and we live with the same terrible hollow in our hearts as do our wives. But males and females do grieve differently. We tell our side of the story in hopes we can provide some solace and direction for other bereaved fathers.

Our wives have said we are less demonstrative than they in our grief, and that is certainly so when we are in public. But given the opportunity to air our feelings in a private discussion among ourselves, without our wives present, we vent, we yell, we stomp out of the room, we argue, we commiserate with one another, we comfort one another, and here and there we shed a tear.

As an aside, it should be noted that, in sharp contrast to our wives, while we chatted around a dinner table laden with food, we ate less and hardly even noticed what we were eating. Comfort food is far more important to women than it is to men. And when the bull session on which this chapter is based ended, we found we could have gone on talking for hours more. We believe there is much to be gained by grieving dads allowing their feelings to emerge unabashedly when surrounded by kindred spirits.

We began our discussion, as did our wives in the first chapter of this book, by revisiting our initial emotions during that first nightmare year. Those feelings remain grotesquely chiseled into our hearts and minds as if forged with a hatchet. We remember every detail and every nuance. At the outset, we each attempted to speak without interrupting each other, but soon found ourselves jumping in wherever and whenever we could with our own diverse thoughts and views. We run it here as it all played out.

*Irv Cohen: "In the beginning I couldn't understand how the world was going on without Jess, when I knew for a fact that the world had stopped. I woke up in the morning and saw cars driving and people walking and I just couldn't believe it. I felt sheer pain as if someone had thrust a sword right through my stomach."*

*Don Barkin: "Lisa was sick for about ten years, so I didn't go through shock. It was a tough period we were going through and it's tough to bring myself back to that time. I was just totally angry. I was angry at Lisa that she died, although I didn't blame her. She had been sick for so long and fought it for so long and at the end I felt she gave up a little. She went and had an operation that she knew was very dangerous. But she was twenty-seven, married, and had a life of her own. The doctors wanted her to have a general anesthetic because she had to have four toes removed. We warned her against it. Any time she'd had general anesthesia before, she'd always gotten fluid down her lungs. The doctor said it had to be done that way, but still we didn't want him to do it. I was so angry. I loved her to pieces, but I was so angry that she did that to herself."*

*Mike Eisenberg: "I start counting from the time Brian was diagnosed with a rare, aggressive form of leukemia. Even though he was a fighter, deep inside I was preparing for the worst. We'd go from crisis to crisis and each time I saw him growing weaker and weaker, and I knew the likelihood of him surviving was getting smaller and smaller. But on the outside, I needed to stay strong for Brian, for his sister and for Barbara. When he died, I felt exhausted. I separated myself from my emotions and moved from my heart to my head. Whatever feeling remained I channeled into rage, and I raged against everything, but especially against God. I put up a kind of fortress and I didn't want anyone to see the suffering inside. I thought if others saw it, I'd have to look at it myself. Early on, in that first year, I heard I would need support from other people, maybe from other men who had similar situations. But I thought, 'That's not me . . . I'm different from you guys.' Yeah, yeah."*

*Joe Colletti: "I had retired that August, bought myself a new car. My son Marc had gotten married in June . . . and then all Hell broke loose. I was angry at God. Not that I was a truly religious person. I was brought up Catholic, but I became a nonbeliever when those two policemen came to tell us. I said, 'It can't be.' When we came home from the morgue, I tried to understand what went on. I said, 'We can't do this by ourselves, we need help.' I'd never asked for help from anybody. During the wake, I went to the deli and I couldn't understand why the people were standing up. It was surreal and absurd. But that's what comes to mind, that people had no right to be standing up. When everybody left and we were left with ourselves and our tears and our screams, we cried so hard that our bodies would ache. We survived on only water and each lost ten pounds. We would just drink a pitcher of water in our bedroom; the bedroom became the dining room. Lorenza went back to work after two weeks, but I was retired and I was going crazy. I was alone and I mostly had nightmares. I would stay in bed until 11 or 12. I couldn't focus on anything for two minutes."*

*Tom Volpe: "I still remember the police at the door at 4 A.M. Instantly, I felt a split in my body. This was too much for me to deal with or comprehend. I guess that was shock. That first year was characterized by feelings that I had no tools to deal with this horror. Rita had lost her father and knew something about bereavement, but I had never lost anybody close to me. My drug of choice became anger. As long as I was angry, I was comfortable. I was angry at anything, angry with God because he had my son. I used to say to God, 'Show your face.' I went to the cemetery two or three times a day. I became self-defeating. I guess your self-esteem suffers. My anger and not dealing with what was going on . . . I guess I was in denial. Denial is not such a bad thing. I had to keep busy; I had enormous energy. I never got tired. In the second year, it got even worse."*

*Bob Long:* "*Michael had been sick for quite a while. We were just sort of going along I guess, so when the event came it was quite a shock. There's really no way to explain it. I had a cacophony of feelings that made every part of my body ache. Everything you believed up to that point, whether religious or philosophical or social, is totally shattered. You have no more beliefs in life because if the worst thing ever can happen to you, then the world is upside down. We reacted in fashion. . . . When I say 'we' I mean that we all had a problem when we grieved at different rates and levels, and some caused discord and some brought us closer. But it's very difficult. You can't criticize anyone about how they grieve; you just have to be there for them, which is tough for men. You have an additional burden, your own and your spouse's. I guess that's a man's way of thinking. We were totally debilitated, physically and mentally. Our lives were upside down and in slow motion. We could step out of them and watch ourselves go through the day. It was surreal. It was total disbelief. It was as if someone had plucked us out of our situation and landed us in some foreign country where people spoke a different language. We withdrew into ourselves. In terms of anger, I'm angry to this day.*"

*Mel Levine:* "*It was like in the movies when that telephone call comes. We found our way to New Jersey. Nurses and doctors came. It was like a movie script. They brought her down and blood was coming out of her nose . . . terrible. I cried from the moment I got into the car until we got home. I'm an angry guy, but I wasn't angry for two years. I didn't have the strength. I didn't want to go to business. It was terrible. I don't remember how I did anything, how I got into a car and drove anywhere. How did I come this distance? It was frightening. I couldn't remember anything. I didn't reach out to anybody. Phyllis did. I've got to give her credit.*"

*Bruce Goldstein:* "*It's a combination of disbelief and denial and then you would find yourself asking 'why'? In our particular case, we don't know the details of why and what happened to Howie. We went through hiring a private investigator and speaking with the police. We think the police kind of sluffed it off as just another college kid at a fraternity weekend. The scenario never made sense to us. Nobody knows and we'll never know. It's different when you know the reason is an illness or an accident. We've just added an additional why or how or what to it. In that first year, I imagined I saw him just over there, and then over there didn't turn out to be anything. Your mind created mirages. I'd go through various scenarios of why he disappeared and why he would come back, almost as if I were writing a Hollywood movie about this person who was needed by the government to do secret work with his unique skills and it would be temporary and everybody would be angry and cry and then continue on with their lives. You know that's not going to happen, but you find your mind wandering because what has really happened is totally unacceptable. You fight with that."*

Cliff Kasden is the only stepfather among our group. He came into the household when Neill was eight years old. Not being the biological father of the deceased child, makes for an entirely different perspective . . . not necessarily an easier one, but very different.

*Cliff Kasden: "I accepted the role of caretaker of the two boys. I was trying to make my way. There was a lot of contention with Neill's natural father, which didn't stop until Neill died and this whole new chapter in life began for everybody. Personally, I experienced a lot of pain. I was there because of Maddy, and now the old Maddy was gone. Watching her was one thing and another was examining my relationship with Neill. He had been very loyal to his natural father. I had my best moments with Neill only when his natural father couldn't provide for him, like when I had to drive him to New Jersey for computer components. But as he grew older, he didn't feel the same obligation to his natural father and so our relationship was getting better. I suffered the loss of what could have been with Neill and, of course, what had been between Maddy and I was gone as well. I still feel a lot of pain as does everybody in this room. Mine may be for different reasons, but I'm in constant pain. In that first year, thank God, Maddy had a job to go to. I became sort of her caretaker, just trying to get her through the next day. I thought maybe I could go forward and find the silver lining wherever that was. I said things like, 'We can't go anyplace, so we won't incur new debts.' As a stepfather instead of inheriting a family and being able to joke around with other fathers who have kids, suddenly I didn't have instant family; I had instant pain. No, I didn't go through shock, because it wasn't my flesh and blood. I'm just shackled with perpetual pain."*

The man who was Neill Perri's flesh and blood father, John Perri, had been divorced from Maddy Kasden for eighteen years prior to their son Neill's death. John had remarried after long years of bachelorhood, and he and his second wife Mary were to become the parents of a baby

girl just ten months following Neill's passing. Still, he had always remained close to Neill and saw him on a weekly basis. He was much involved with Neill's life. John lived nearby and was there throughout the
events surrounding Neill's death and burial. After some initial reluctance
to share his feelings for the purpose of this book, John agreed, ultimately
deciding that his views would be relevant to divorced fathers whose
children have died after the divorce. He was not at the meeting with the
other fathers, but spoke later of his feelings.

*John Perri: "There was probably some ambivalence on my part, one side of
me wanting to talk to you and the other side of me not. My way is kind of the
opposite of what Maddy and her group do. They're continually reaching out to do
things for parents who've lost children, reaching out to give back and help . . .
but I think they're also doing it for their own needs. I could never do what they
do. I would just die inside.*

*"As much as they are in it and live with it all the time, I kind of run the
other way. It's my way of dealing with it to an extent. When Neill died I
couldn't face it, so it was fortuitous that I was married and with a different family. And then Mary's pregnancy a month later was a gift from God and made it
a little easier.*

*"Mary was able to give me love and sympathy without suffering in the same
way I was. I think a husband and wife who have lost a child are both in the same
hole. You want to help each other, but you're both twenty feet in a hole. It's easier in a situation where there's a stepmother. Mary didn't know Neill that well.
She was upset about him, but she could give more of herself; she wasn't hurting
the way I was.*

*"Also there was the timing of my daughter's birth. I think we found out
Mary was pregnant two months after Neill died. In one way, it was difficult dealing with all those mixed emotions about life and death, which was bizarre in and
of itself, but on the other hand I had something new and a new life. So, that gave
me something else to focus on. I was able to continue my life and if I say 'move
on' it's a poor term, because you can never really move on from that experience.
But I could continue my life and do things."*

In the first chapter of this book, our wives described the terrible exhaustion they all felt in that first year following the deaths of our chil-

dren. Our wives wanted nothing more than to curl up and sleep so as to block out all thought. They each fell victim to enormous mental and physical fatigue, and just getting up for the day was almost more than they could bear. They were drained of energy. Not so most of us. Our anger seemed to fuel our energy.

*Irv:* "*I had a need to work at a furious pace. I ripped up all the posts in my fence and concreted them all. I scraped and painted the house and stayed as busy as I could.*"

*Don:* "*Within the terrible anger that I felt, I also built up strength to keep moving. I didn't stop. I just wanted to go. When Carol couldn't go to work, I dragged her out of the house and made her come to work. For me, the only solution was just to keep going. I wanted to bury myself in work and not think about what happened.*"

*Mike:* "*I returned to work and tried to stay focused. It was okay as long as I kept going. If I slowed down, I thought I would never have the energy to start again. Move, constantly move. Eventually, the ache deep inside me took it's toll and I stopped working.*"

*Joe:* "*With Lorenza back at work and me being retired, I had to do something. On television, I saw a group of women who were sculpting in an adult education program at the high school. I called up the television station and a very compassionate lady gave me the number to call. I lost myself in the sculpting. Marc died on the water. I made fish, fish, fish; I made dolphins. I gave them to family. That was my therapy. I would sculpt; the ladies were talking of their children and grandchildren. I couldn't talk about my child. Eventually in class, my voice got a little stronger and I had a little more energy.*"

*Bruce:* "*I went back to work a week after sitting shiva with the hope that work would give me something to hide behind. It didn't really and after a few years, I completely lost interest and didn't care. The economy had turned bad and the business needed more thought and energy than I could give it. I gave my partner a year's notice. I felt it was time to get out and make changes, even if it meant doing nothing. And it did. Now I help Barbara with the bookkeeping for her business, but nothing really structured.*

"*As far as being tired, I was tired, but no it doesn't end in that first year. Are you forever tired? Yeah. You're investing so much energy in just getting yourself up and trying to function at some level close to where you were before the death of your child. I'm sure some of the fatigue is periodic bouts with depression. Every now and then, you'd find yourself tired of feeling tired. It starts to wear you down that you're always feeling worn down."*

*Tom: "My office was still operating. I went there, but I was incapable of making any decisions. I fought with everybody. A couple of years later, I closed down the office. By that time I had no more staff; I had fought with them all."*

Whereas our wives spoke of wanting to die and having nothing to live for, we never heard them actually say they contemplated suicide. A couple of us, however, did actually think of taking our own lives. One of us tried and failed. Whether or not we thought to kill ourselves following the deaths of our children, we have all come to know death in a decidedly different light or a different shadow . . . depending on the day.

*Mel: "I didn't contemplate suicide. But I wasn't afraid of death."*

*Mike: "I wanted to be with Brian. I would scream in my head that I couldn't stand my life. But would I take my own life? I never answered that question."*

*Bob: "We didn't talk about suicide. I didn't think my son would want us to. We want to live, but we're not afraid. We have a closer relationship with death."*

*Don: "The same with me. Lisa did not even want us at the hospital when we had a vacation planned. She always wanted us to continue living. I never contemplated suicide."*

*Tom: "Maybe I was suicidal for a while, but I don't think I really ever contemplated suicide. I was very reckless."*

*Joe: "Some time after Marc died, I had to order a casket for my father. I already had a relationship by then with death. It was the same thing. I'd been through it."*

Our wives felt enormous guilt and the majority of us also harbored unrelenting guilt. In some ways we men—the stronger sex, according to the upbringing of our generation—felt even greater responsibility for what happened than did our spouses.

What we have learned collectively about the guilt we felt then and in some cases continue to feel is that we have been handed a lot in life for which we were never trained. We could never have prepared ourselves for how we should or should not act upon losing a child. It is important to try to forgive yourself and cut yourself some slack. Unfortunately, that is easier said than done.

Much of the blame we take upon ourselves is, of course, totally irrational, but we are not dealing with a rational state of affairs here. One of the words we often use, and have used in this book repeatedly, to describe what we have been through is "surreal." When the place you are coming from is surreal, any nightmarish emotion or reaction is possible . . . even probable.

*Mel: "Supposing I didn't give Andrea a stick-shift car. Supposing I'd given her an automatic car, would this accident have occurred?"*

*Don: "The guilt I felt and still feel was not being able to stop Lisa from doing what I knew was not right for her, having that general anesthesia. Carol and I knew it was not good for her to have it, but she was a married adult. Still it's guilt. I say to myself that if I'd exercised stronger influence maybe she would have lived a little longer."*

*Tom: "When you talk of guilt everybody brings their own baggage. Michael died in an auto accident. I was car crazy, I used to race cars, I still am car crazy. And I still smoke after my father died of lung cancer. Isn't that insane? I taught Michael how to drive; I set poor examples for him because he liked to be crazy with the car, too. I didn't do my job. I didn't teach him enough safety behind the wheel. It was absolutely my fault and I couldn't fix it. Then after a few days my dog died. My wife and son were falling apart. They brought a priest into the house to bless it and rid it of evil spirits. Where were my tools to fix this? All my life I'd been lucky, I was able to fix things. . . . I couldn't fix this."*

*Irv: "I felt guilt because just before the accident, my brother-in-law-asked if he should stop the boat because we were getting to the end of the lake. I said, 'Make a turn to the left,' and that's the way we went. It was one aspect that I've had to live with. Even worse, I couldn't spare Audrey the pain. I realized she was hurting even more than me."*

*Don: "I think the hardest thing for me is that men put themselves in the role of protectors; that's our job. We try to help our wives with their pain, but I couldn't help Carol. I felt so helpless and useless. It was a very, very difficult time for me until I realized that there was no way in Hell I could help her. It took me about two or three years before I realized I couldn't help her."*

Mike: "I still carry around a lot of baggage for so many reasons. Now that we are talking about it, I guess I felt omnipotent. I selected a medical specialty that gave me an illusion of being in control. I was used to running an operating room and things were done just so and were so rigid. And then I was so disappointed in the care that Brian got. First I was a physician, then an anesthesiologist and a pain reliever and I couldn't do any of those things for Brian. I had the illusion that maybe if I could see that every little thing was done properly, he'd stand a chance of surviving. I still feel I could have done more and if I had, maybe. But who do I think I am? That's part of my baggage."

Joe: "We introduce our children to nature and it's a positive thing. What's wrong with that? We teach them to enjoy the backyard, bugs, growing things, fishing. He always used to tease me. I would go fishing with him, but I would never really fish. I introduced him to fishing. It was a very innocent thing. He bought a boat before he bought a car. Maybe if I hadn't introduced him to that.

"I was always concerned about him being on a small boat. One time there was an accident not involving Man and I called him to kind of warn him. He said he'd heard about it and he thanked me. That's all I could do. You second guess yourself, like Monday night quarterbacking. But at the end of the day, he was an adult, he had a wife, he loved the sea and that's what took him."

Bob: "Luckily I didn't feel guilt. I didn't think I had control over what happened to Michael. At Compassionate Friends we talked to people in similar situations. Half of them felt guilty because they didn't have their child go through a bone-marrow transplant. The other camp said they felt guilty because they did. They couldn't both be right, and that kind of unburdened us from our decision. It was a big help not to have the guilt to obscure the rest of the problems."

Bruce: "Guilt? No, I never really experienced that. Only regrets one or two times that I should have done something differently after Howie was injured. Like I wish I had sat by his side every second of the thirty hours he survived in the hospital. I couldn't feel guilt that I let him go off to school and most of the time didn't know what he was doing. He was twenty-one, there was no reason for him to check in with us every few seconds. In listening to a lot of people speak at meetings and such, a lot of that guilt comes from a feeling they were judged by

*God, that they were being punished for some inadequacy on their part. In my mind, I hear them and I sit there screaming quietly, 'What kind of a God is this that goes after your child because of something you did wrong?' This is not a God that I would ever accept, but then I'm not much of a believer."*

What of God? Have we lost whatever faith we may have had before the deaths of our children? Do we blame God? Do we continue to practice religion?

*Bruce: "Having a strong belief in God is both a positive and a minus. Because if you're like Barbara, who had a much stronger religious belief than me, you felt betrayed. You do what you've been brought up to do and therefore everything should be fine. When it's not fine, another anchor is pulled from beneath you. If you don't have that anchor going in, you can't lose it. I went to temple on Yom Kippur, which falls right around when Howie died, and I saw all these people coming up and donating pledge money to the temple and telling of how they had this or that illness or a relative did and they prayed and did the right thing and everything turned out okay. I'm thinking, it doesn't always turn out okay. Would these folks be praising God if their story ended with a death?"*

*Bob: "I went to Catholic school and was heavy into theology. After my son died, I decided they were full of shit. It just can't happen this way. Somebody is wrong, and I've got the proof. When you read what various religions say about death, they all have diverse opinions. There's no cohesive way to treat death. Even the mainstream religions don't know. So, they can't all be right."*

*Joe: "I don't believe what happened to Marc was written in the big book somewhere. I don't believe it was destined. I used to think you were rewarded for doing good, but all that was turned upside down. I was very angry with a counselor at church. She said when we are born again we have a brand-new body. She quoted the pope. I said I just wanted my old son back."*

*Cliff: "I accepted what happened. I never hated God. I was brought up with strong faith, and I was never taught that God owed me anything. Maddy wasn't raised with that understanding of God, which was unfortunate. I wish she had been. I understood that if you were a good boy it didn't mean you got presents from God and that helped me a lot."*

*Mel: "I went to a rabbi and he couldn't explain it. I went into a church and found a bishop and he said he understood. He had lost a daughter. He said, 'God wanted your daughter in heaven.' That kept me docile for two years and then I got angry again."*

Tom: *"I would have hit the bishop."*

We railed against God and we railed against formal institutions, we railed against the doctors who treated our children and we railed against society in general. We just didn't care anymore, and much of that stony apathy has stayed with us over the years. Our priorities are forever changed.

Bob: *"I had a tremendous distrust and reversal in my feelings about institutions. I even hated the public library for six months. I remember driving past a gas station, which had a person in an Easter bunny costume standing outside waving to passersby. I gave him the finger. The world just cannot continue as it was because it has changed irrevocably. I've totally withdrawn and become devoid of social niceties. Like if I walk into a store and hear people agonizing over the color of a fabric . . . should it be blue or green . . . I want to hit them over the head with a chair. One benefit is that I've learned to say no. People ask would I like to do this or that. I say no. It's like having money in a bank account. But, I don't have any emotional capital to give; it's gone, it's spent. I have to take care of me first. If that goes, I might as well be a vegetable."*

Don: *"Lisa had a lot of doctors in the ten years or so she was sick. She was in maybe six or seven hospitals. I can only recall one doctor who was really compassionate. I could tell you weeks of stories of doctors who wouldn't listen to us because we were laymen, but we had seen what she was going through for years."*

Bob: *"That may be true, but we're all angry at the medical profession because they couldn't save our kids. Our anger centers on them."*

Mike: *"There were many compassionate people around Brian, but to this date I still remember the faces of those who failed to ease his suffering. I'm angry that they ignored Brian the young man and instead focused on his horrible disease."*

Bruce: *"There was a young neurosurgical resident who was involved in Howie's case and with him at the end. Just minutes after Howie died, we met him leaving the elevator and laughing with some other interns. His expression quickly changed when he saw us. I wondered how you become so callous so quickly, especially after handling the death of a young man, almost your contemporary."*

Don: *"Those doctors who have a heart, have a heart. Those who clinically don't have a heart, never will. Maybe they're in the wrong profession."*

Joe: *"Maybe they're incapable of showing their sensitivity."*

Don: *"Then they shouldn't be there. . . . It's part of what makes the patient get better."*

Did we rail against our wives as well? How did our marriages fare from our points of view?

Irv: *"I think there's a natural inclination to want to be closer. But a lot of times Audrey's depression has been a problem. Now she's gone back on antidepressants and she's back to being herself; I feel much more loving and amorous toward her. For a time, her grief was so bad that I'd walk into the house and feel she was loaded for bear. All I had to do was open my mouth and she let me have it."*

Mike: *"Barbara didn't want to go on antidepressants. She wanted to feel the pain and it went on and on and on. It pushed us further apart. I couldn't stand watching her pain. I needed to isolate myself until one day she decided she would take medication and then the real Barbara reappeared."*

Tom: *"I was angry and we had problems, but my wife is the only woman who knew Michael. I can't say that we're closer or further apart. We live more separate lives than we did then. We're at different stages in our lives, we were caught up in raising our children, now we're at a different place. We are not really living our lives at our capacity, as we should be. We don't travel. I would like to buy a boat. We seem stuck."*

Bruce: *"We never separated or anything, but it depends on how you define separate ways. At the end of the day, in that first year especially, Barbara wanted to be alone. She would go off into one part of the house and I would go off into another. She would fall asleep wherever she was and I on the couch where I was. It wasn't so much going away from the other person as it was wanting to be alone with our thoughts, and not having the energy to have more than the thoughts which were focused on Howie. We sought out counseling when we saw the mind-boggling statistics of bereaved couples that had broken up completely, a 90 percent break-up rate."*

*Cliff:* "*There's not a day goes by that Maddy and I don't fight, but I think that's pretty normal. What my snapshot was when I moved in was, 'Wow, I have a great woman and an instant family. We'll work out this other thing with the other father.' That's not what panned out. But I respect myself and my sense of what I want to do. I make the choice. If I hated it so much, nothing is stopping me from walking out the door. And my choice to stay says everything. If I'm going to stay then I have to accept everything and make the changes I can make. I'm the third parent, which puts me in a less potent position. That's the choice and that's the deal that I've got and that's what I'm going to play. I love Maddy and she loves me and I loved Neill as much as he would let me, and that's what I play with. The pain is real and waking up with the same anguish as the other dads is real and it's my choice to stick it out.*"

*Don:* "*I give you a lot of credit. A lot of men would have walked out. You're dealing with a tough situation. Her anguish is the biggest part of your life.*"

We asked each other whether mothers or fathers feel greater pain after the loss of a child, and then we asked each other if we could even offer up judgment on such a topic. We agreed and we disagreed. Some of us maintained that because our wives physically carried the child for nine months, delivered the child, and were the primary nurturers during the developing years, a mother and child bond was created that could not be equaled in a father and child relationship. Others disagreed heartily, saying they felt a closeness that in several cases was even greater than the ties between their child and their wife. We concurred that certainly women invest greater time and energy in raising a child, while men act as the protectors and providers. But we differed on whether any of that would necessarily translate into a greater love. We felt that dissimilar relationships evolved simply from raising daughters or sons. There is always that "guy thing" to consider.

*Joe:* "*I feel bad when I think of promises unfulfilled, of joys not shared, of what could have been but never will be. I inherited tools and a pocket watch from my father and he from his father. Who shall inherit these now? With whom can I share the joy, the euphoria, if the Giants win the Superbowl?*"

And then we argued that to say even that was to generalize. Obviously, we are not of one mind on the issue.

We became acquainted with one another through the same channel in which our wives met, the Compassionate Friends bereavement group. Some of us were led to Compassionate Friends by our wives, some of us led our wives there. We also have been to bereavement counselors, marriage counselors and psychics. Several of us were helped by these various avenues, others were not.

But we have all found it necessary to commune with other bereaved parents. Whether it be in an organized format or not, everybody needs someone to talk to, and only those who are speaking the same language—in this case the language of the parent who has lost a child—can hold a truly relevant discourse.

*Bob: "Talking to people who are not aggrieved is akin to someone giving you a cookbook when you have a flat tire. They mean well, but it doesn't help."*

*Bruce: "We went to a support group and a private bereavement counselor who met with a few couples at one time. It was helpful in that you got a chance to say what was on your mind, and even if you were not verbal, you could identify with what somebody said. With Compassionate Friends and other groups, you find others have the same feelings, that you are not crazy or that your partner's feelings are not some aberration that is so far out of what can be expected that you have to worry about the mental health of the individual. It's drummed into you that each bereaved person is going down this track at their own speed, and while you all reach the various stations on that track, you reach them at different times. Some people stop at one station longer than others and then they move on.*

*"Basically a support group is a validation of what you're thinking and feeling, and that's where it's most helpful. For some people, it becomes a way of life and almost a substitute for the nearness of your child."*

*Joe: "The first people we phoned were the Compassionate Friends. We read about them in a magazine. They came right over."*

*Bob: "We were led to Compassionate Friends. It was a roadmap after the first couple of meetings when we just looked at the floor. The only relief is when you are with the Compassionate Friends."*

*Mel: "Phyllis took me to Compassionate Friends; truthfully, I got nothing out of it."*

*Mike: "Toward the end of the first year, I started to fall apart. I needed support from people and Compassionate Friends helped me to realize I wasn't going crazy and that other men had similar situations. It was comforting to be in the middle of something supportive. I'd never had that feeling before."*

*Tom: "I remember attending a bereavement conference in North Carolina. I went in laughing with a friend. The seminar was on guilt. This woman was telling about losing her two children in a fire that was her fault. She'd put a cloth over a lampshade because the lamp was too bright. The facilitator talked of how he'd picked up a prescription a doctor had prescribed for his daughter who was sick. It was the wrong dosage and his daughter died. He blamed himself for not checking the label, for not tasting the medicine. It was all irrational, but he blamed himself; he became an alcoholic, he lost his job, his wife left him. I started to talk about my own guilt and fifteen minutes after I walked in laughing, I'm crying uncontrollably. I wasn't that different from that man. I had been denying my feelings. That meeting brought them to the surface."*

*Joe: "We used to go to the Compassionate Friends meetings and it was very draining. It would cause a sleepless night, but still it helped you to identify and find you were not going nuts. There's a camaraderie in that."*

*Tom: "I hardly ever attend Compassionate Friends meetings now, but when I get talking with a group like this a funny thing happens. . . . this is starting to hurt. I used to get into my angry mode, now I switch into a gratitude mode. I went to a therapist; he said the only way out of this anger is through gratitude. It stuck with me. I could have remained angry the rest of my life and destroyed my marriage. I had my son for twenty years. My life changed when I had him and my life changed again when he died. I grew up with his death. I have to tell myself that to stay out of pain."*

*Joe: "My daughter sent me to a psychologist and then a psychiatrist. He said I didn't have clinical depression, that I was just grieving greatly. He asked if I wanted a little Prozac to please my daughter. I said yes. I took it and gave it to somebody else. I think they gave it to their dog."*

*Bruce: "We went a couple of times to the psychic. You go there with half of you saying this is a charlatan, that it's smoke and mirrors, and part of you saying it's got to be right because I'll take any avenue to see, smell, feel my child again. Some of what they say you can sluff off as a good interviewer giving back to you most of the information you give them. But there are a few parts where they have no reason to know. It gives you something to hang on to; it's temporary to a great extent, but you suddenly feel there is a next step and you will meet up with your child and spend all eternity with them. That goes away after awhile, and your logical more earthly self comes out.*

*"The second time we went to a psychic, we walked in and in less than thirty seconds he said, 'Your son is showing me his name as a question mark.' Well, we always referred to Howie as How. Another psychic told us she saw the letter H on my face. So you can intellectually debunk 95 percent of it, the other 5 percent can either give you cause for concern or cause for hope, whatever way you are feeling."*

Don: *"Carol claims to talk to Lisa when she meditates, but I don't believe in it. I'm at a different level. I know when Carol sees certain signs she believes in that. It's important to her."*

Much like our wives, we are keyed in to seeing signs and keeping mementos.

Irv: *"Jess and I had a song. One day, as I came to work, I was feeling really down and I pulled into my parking spot. Just before I cut the engine, I said, 'Jessie, talk to me, tell me you're okay.' Just then our song came on. About a year later, I was driving on a rainy, miserable night and I was in a terrible funk. Once again, the exact same thing happened. There were only two times I called out for Jessie to talk to me, and both times the song came on. Another time, I went to the cemetery with Audrey. I had been reluctant to go, but as I stepped out of the car I found a pin on the ground with a J and an angel sitting on it."*

Bruce: *"The butterfly is something a lot of grief groups hang on to. It's fragile, beautiful, and has an extremely short life span. Everybody finds something they take as a signal that their child is there. We hear a certain song that we feel is Howie's way of coming through to us and letting us know he's around. I think everybody grabs at that."*

But others of us are more pragmatic. We can feel their presence without seeing direct signs.

Don: *"I wouldn't say there isn't anything to signs. But I don't think it's our children talking to us. I think it's more us looking for things. My wife is al-*

*ways on the lookout for things to tie us to Lisa. She looks for butterflies. But but-*
*terflies fly past me all the time. They land on my shoulder on the golf course.*
*That's what butterflies do. Is that my daughter talking to me? I don't think so. I*
*think you have to want to believe in that."*

Tom: *"I read once that death does not end a relationship, it changes it. I have*
*a whole new relationship with Michael. I feel he's with me and I'm never alone.*
*We knew each other pretty well, Mike and I, and I really feel I still have a good*
*relationship with him. He's not far."*

Our wives seem to become more upset than we do about insensitive remarks made by unthinking outsiders. Surely we hear them, and we are taken aback momentarily by the stupidity of some of their comments, but we tend to more quickly dismiss them as well.

Bob: *" 'Civilians' think they can solve your problem or give advice because*
*they assume problems have a beginning, a middle and an end. But grief never*
*ends; it just changes. It's always there. 'Civilians' think they can give you a so-*
*lution when there is no solution."*

Mel: *"They say they know how I feel. How do they know how I feel? You*
*just dismiss it out of hand."*

Bruce: *"Most of us have heard those worthless platitudes all our lives. One*
*individual went on and on about his ninety-year-old mother who had died. Here*
*I was just trying to get off the chair, having lost my twenty-one-year-old son, and*
*he was carrying on and on. But part of me realized he had his sorrow and was*
*totally within himself at that juncture. Mostly, people would ask me what hap-*
*pened to Howie and when I told them I didn't know how he died, there wasn't*
*any place else for the conversation to go."*

Even with the passage of time, our worlds remain colorless. To the outsider, we appear to be no different than anyone else. But scratch the surface and grief is always there.

We have a newly acquired sensitivity to the pain of others. When others are bereaved, we seem to take it unto ourselves and make it part of our own existence. We have been there.

Mike: *"I'm certain I have something to give to someone else who has lost*
*children. Just being there for them. The day is worthwhile if I can take some of*

*my pain and suffering and turn it around and have someone else's pain diminished."*

Tom: *"I share that feeling with you."*

We look at the monuments and memorials that have risen in memory of the victims of the September 11 terrorist attacks. We know that those monuments may help the non-bereaved to put in perspective what happened and reach their own "closure." But for the parents and spouses, the sisters, brothers and children of the victims, monuments mean very little. Again, there is no closure.

Bruce: *"Monuments are so other people can see the loss. The victims' families go home with their loss."*

Mike: *"I just returned from the funeral of a close friend who was murdered. I've been to other funerals since Brian died. This was really the first time I allowed myself to feel the deep loss. I was crying. This friend died before his time and that's what happened to our children. I couldn't stop crying in the church."*

Bob: *"The families of the 9/11 victims had their grief capitalized on. Ours was not. In one instance, friends of my wife's were staging a fund-raiser for a very sick man. He spoiled their plans by dying before they could hold it. So they simply changed the name of the event and carried on, business is business. It was totally mind-boggling the way they could write off a human being in that way."*

With time, we have even learned to enjoy ourselves . . . upon occasion. We laugh, we travel, we anticipate some event with hopeful expectation. We have resumed some of the activities we enjoyed prior to our children's deaths, but without the same enthusiasm.

Irv: *"I went back to tennis almost immediately. It was a distraction, going through the motions to keep occupied."*

Mel: *"I play tennis. Someone came and got me after six months, which was a very long time for me."*

Don: *"I enjoy myself now. But in the beginning I was miserable, burying myself in my work. There were months that went by that I don't recall at all. But the next year, I started to play golf again . . . slowly . . . at first I couldn't get my head into it."*

Mike: *"I enjoy woodworking. I just immerse myself in the wood and the tools and the peace. It's very peaceful."*

*Joe:* "*I feel more at peace when I am with this group here. I enjoy my art class, the sculpture. If not for Marc, I would never have pursued that. I always thought I might want to do it, but Marc's death pushed me to do it.*"

*Cliff:* "*I never stopped doing the things that made me happy . . . reading Sherlock Holmes, the Yankees. I don't feel euphoria if they win, but I feel happy. A lot that happens to me is contingent on how Maddy is feeling. So, if she's doing well one week, I can sort of ease up on myself and feel a bit better. Yesterday she found some Sherlock Holmes coins for me, and that meant a lot to me; she was thinking of me for a change and not wallowing in her grief. It was a good sign.*"

*Bruce:* "*I play golf. It's a good escape and all consuming at the moment. But so much that was important before is not now. I used to be a sports nut, now I couldn't care less about the teams. My concentration ability never came back to what it was.*"

But we try to move on. Our families grow. Life improves and grows more complicated.

*Bruce:* "*We were in the house and the neighborhood for thirty-two years. It held nothing but triggers of our past life. We took turns wanting to get out and said if we both reach that point at the same time then we would move. That was coupled with the fact that the housing market went sky high and our two surviving sons were living in Connecticut. Now we are there, too. It's worked out positively because while we walk around the house and have all the same photos on the wall and the same memories in our heads, it's not the place where everything happened.*

"*We have a grandson nearby now. He's adorable. You can love again. It's something that just happens that you may not believe will ever happen again. You almost have to steel yourself against getting close to somebody again because you've been burned so badly. But if you were a loving person before, there's every likelihood you'll become a loving person again, in spite of your fears . . . especially when they put this little baby in front of you and he looks just like his father, our eldest son, at that age. You bond very quickly. But, of course, whatever I say there will be cases that prove me wrong.*"

We know that our wives think a great deal about someday seeing our children again. We are not as absorbed in the thought as they are, and we try to differentiate between reality and fantasy. But neither are we altogether willing to take a chance and rule out the possibility of a reunion with our sons and daughters.

Mike: *"There's that slim hope."*

Bob: *"It's a very strong pull. The son of an acquaintance of mine died. When I called to offer my sympathies the only words he could muster were, 'Bob, please tell me . . . am I ever going to see him again?' I said yes, because that was his main focus. He had to perpetuate that hope."*

Tom: *"There is a spirit world, we just don't deal with it everyday."*

Joe: *"How do you measure that?"*

Tom: *"When I die, I don't think I'll see my son as I knew him as a human being. But I think we will connect spiritually. It's funny, even now sometimes I don't feel that I've lost Michael. I have a pretty good relationship with him. Certainly, I've lost him in the physical sense, but for that matter, I haven't lost my father, my grandfather, my aunts, either.*

Joe: *"You're talking of what you remember of them."*

Mel: *"I don't talk to Andrea. I think of her. I really don't think I'll see her again. It's a fantasy."*

Joe: *"I can't talk to Marc. The telephone has been disconnected."*

Bruce: *"Will I see my child again? You want to keep that feeling that you'll come across him or her to hug them or throttle them or both. You have to hang on to that crutch. It's what stiffens your legs and your backbone in the morning, so that you can get out of bed."*

## Ten

# The Siblings Speak

Ont of the first things people ask when they hear that our parents lost a child is, "Do they have any other children?" We are . . . "the other children."

We have heard ourselves described as "forgotten mourners," and in some respects that is so. When our siblings died, we were young adults. We were not tiny tots clutching the hand of a grown-up or weighted down by our fallen brother's fire hat at his funeral. The world was too moved to notice that we, too, were in mourning.

As we stood shocked and trying to come to terms with the horror of our brother's or sister's death, we were admonished to "be strong for your parents." We were expected to take on a mantle of maturity for which no one is prepared.

*Wendy Barkin Sutkin (Wendy was twenty-five when her sister Lisa died):*

"*Everyone came to pay a condolence call and everyone said, 'Make sure you are good for your parents.' Hello, what about me?*"

Tom Volpe (*Tom was eighteen when his brother Michael died*): "*I was trying to keep it together as much as possible for the sake of my parents, who were just blindsided. I was going through a lot of emotions, but I tried to be the good son and keep it all together.*"

Allegra Colletti (*Allegra was twenty-eight when her brother Marc died*): "*I felt that I apparently didn't exist.*"

Barry Levine (*Barry was twenty-six when his sister Andrea died*): "*You had the enormous responsibility of worrying about your parents, and they couldn't worry about you. I remember telling them I loved them. I took walks around the block with my father. I saw my parents in a different light. They were emotional, crying a lot, I'd never really seen my father cry.*"

Philip Goldstein (*Philip was twenty-four when his brother Howard died*): "*No one ever came to me and said you need to do these things. I was their first-born son, I knew they needed me to do certain things.*"

Some of us were oblivious to what anyone had to say.

Abbe Levine (*Abbe was twenty-nine when her sister Andrea died*): "*I felt pretty numb and may not have been aware of expectations, but I did what I had to do to get through each day.*"

It is not natural for a teen or young adult to lose a sibling. These were the people we laughed with, shared secrets with, the only ones who could see our family from our perspective.

Allegra: "*Marc and I were less than two years apart and as close as you could get to being twins. We were connected, attached. My mother used to call us by the same blended name. I don't remember reality before him. We always looked out for each other and I thought we would eventually grow old together.*"

Tom: "*He was twenty, I was eighteen, there was just the two of us. Everything is different. My grandmother still calls me by his name.*"

Debi Cohen (*Debi was thirty-seven and the mother of three children when her half-sister Jessica died*): "*Jessie could have been my daughter. She was like my fourth child in many ways. She spent her vacations with me and my children.*"

We not only lost a sibling, we lost the parents we had known. In time they might find a "new normal," but they would be forever changed.

*Debi: "It was painful just to look at their faces, their eyes."*

*Wendy: "I remember my mother saying she didn't want to live anymore and it was awful hearing her say that. After that, my parents changed a lot. To this day they are different people, they look at things differently."*

*Abbe: "While I was twenty-nine and knew my parents were human, I wasn't prepared to see how vulnerable they were."*

*Philip: "You are completely destabilized by seeing your parents unravel before your eyes. I don't think it matters how old you are. You always assume your parents are there to be the stability in your life. For many years after Howie died, I saw my parents as sad, in pain and fragile. Over time, things got much better. Today I am amazed that they have found a new normal in their lives that enables them to enjoy travel, retirement, each other and their family."*

Our parents' lives ground to a halt during the first year after the deaths. Yes, they went through the motions of daily living, but they did so almost as automatons. We on the other hand were expected to carry on with our lives much as before.

*Wendy: "Lisa died three months before my wedding. I said I didn't want my wedding, but my father broke down and said Lisa would have wanted it. No one was letting me not have it. They tried to make it still about me and my best day, but I could never watch my wedding video."*

*Barry: "I got married several months after Andrea died. One of the first things my mother said was that I was not to change my wedding plans. In my wedding album my parents have blank stares. They wanted to be at the wedding for me, but they were there with heavy hearts."*

*Tom: "I had been a happy-go-lucky kid a couple of months before, and then I started college three months after he died and I wasn't anymore. They thought I should take some time before I started, but I wanted to go and not feel as if everything in life had just stopped. At school I wouldn't talk about my brother. I turned to drugs for a lot of years. It was a tough time developmentally."*

In their too short lives our brothers and sisters had little time to develop the faults we who have gone on to live have often accumulated. Sometimes it seems that our siblings died pure . . . they were perfect.

And, even if they were not perfect, they oftentimes seem so in our parents' view.

*Allegra: "There can be a lot of revisionist history. It's their version of things and maybe it's not always accurate in my eyes."*

*Tom: "They put him on a pedestal. All events that were not wonderful are simply erased and they only remember the good days. His life will always be written as full of promise, no mistakes . . . he will always be perfect. He wasn't perfect before, brothers know things their parents don't. We rewrite history."*

*Debi: "No, I don't feel that way. My parents have come right out and said that Jess wasn't perfect."*

*Barry: "I don't think my mother and father put Andrea on a pedestal. They speak of her sense of humor and of highlights about her as a person and I'm okay with it."*

Much as our parents have the dilemma of how to answer when people ask, "How many children do you have?" so we, too, must deal with "How many brothers and sisters do you have?"

*Barry: "My decisions are made spontaneously depending on whom I am talking with. If I feel comfortable with the person I will tell them about my sister."*

*Debi: "You self-monitor what you say depending upon the listener. Some people are very sensitive, and we monitor what we say to protect others."*

*Allegra: "In the beginning it was important to me not to deny. I was so afraid that everyone would forget that Marc ever existed. I was adamant about telling people, even if was awkward for both them and me . . . too bad . . . that's the reality, deal with it. Now it's more like, why bother."*

*Wendy: "I don't go into it much. It's easier to just say I had two sisters. People don't really want to know."*

*Tom: "But if you don't mention them, you feel like you're denying them."*

*Philip: "At first I didn't include Howie because I was ducking the follow-up questions. Now I enjoy talking about both my brothers. I also have discovered there are unfortunately many others like me who mourn the death of a sibling."*

Much as we do not share our parents' compelling need to tell people about the child who died, not all of us go repeatedly to the cemetery. When we do go it is usually to mark a certain occasion or for the sake of our parents.

*Wendy:* "*July seventh was my sister's birthday. On that day I take my kids to the cemetery. My older daughter is named after Lisa. I bring them because I feel it's important for them to know of her and her death and to know that I had a sister.*"

*Tom:* "*My parents are at the cemetery all the time and that's great for them. It's how they deal with it. But, I don't want to remember him that way and I don't think he'd want me to remember him that way.*"

*Allegra:* "*Instead, I go to the memorial stone by the water and I look out at the water where he died. Once it seemed as if the water and life went on and on forever.*"

*Barry:* "*It's not the way I want to remember my sister. It works for my mom. She will go and sit and talk to my sister. I feel guilty about that, but it's not for me. My connection is the memories I have.*"

Guilt comes over us in other ways as well.

*Wendy:* "*I found for quite a while I felt guilty about enjoying anything, like when I first got married. She wasn't enjoying life. So there was a lot of guilt. You get over it. I don't feel the same guilt today. That feeling of why am I here and she's not took a year or two to fade away. It becomes an ache in your head instead of the center of everything.*"

*Tom:* "*Sometimes you wish you'd died and maybe they'd be less upset. You think all sorts of crazy things. Doesn't every sibling go through that? But, over time you learn to live with the pain.*"

*Abbe:* "*I feel guilt or something like it that I don't have much memory of my sister or a sense of connection. I wish I could find ways to keep her more alive within me but it has been twenty years.*"

*Philip:* "*Being a constant mourner is exhausting. It made me feel guilty at times that I was dishonoring Howie's memory by coping and moving on with my life. But, I had to.*"

Being young adults, we all had our own circle of friends. Some of us were married, engaged or had significant others. Some of these people understood what we were going through while others did not. We learned to take each situation in stride.

*Debi:* "*I wound up dropping a lot of my closest friends because they disappointed me. They weren't there for me physically or emotionally. It may be that they didn't know what to do or say, but I'm not tolerant of that. Previous to Jessie, I had not been tested as a friend that way, but I'd like to think I'd have made that special effort to be compassionate."*

Barry: *"My wife Patty and I were engaged when Andrea died. Patty was closer to my sister than I was in some ways. They had a certain bonding. Patty is very emotional and she was terrific for my parents and very supportive for me. She was with me when I learned of Andrea's death and she mourned with me."*

Abbe: *"My husband and I were married three months when Andrea died. He was supportive, but it's not easy to live with someone who is sad so much of the time. I know that now, but I wasn't so aware of how hard it was for him at the time."*

Wendy: *"I was engaged at the time. He tried to be there for me, but he didn't know how. I think I just accepted it because I didn't know what else to do. I would cry at night and not be open about it."*

Allegra: *"My then fiancé didn't call for four days after Marc died. He did come to the funeral, but he was clueless, emotionally unavailable. He said he didn't know what to do and didn't want to intrude."*

Allegra's fiancé could offer no further explanation for his reaction. Eventually, the couple went their separate ways. However, his inability to show compassion reminded Allegra that years earlier she, too, had been of little comfort when a friend's mother died.

Allegra: *"I remembered how as a teenager I had been horrible to a friend when her mother died. I didn't understand what was happening. But when my brother died, she was there for me, calling people, inviting them to the funeral. I said not to, but she said you tell people and let them decide for themselves. Later I apologized to her for not being there for her when her mother died."*

Tom: *"At school I wouldn't talk about my brother. I was an escapist."*

Barry: *"A few months after Andrea died, my parents set up a memorial fund in her name at a children's hospital. On what would have been her fortieth birthday, my mother asked me to send letters to my friends regarding the fund. I was disappointed with the contributions we received and I had words with some of my friends. I wanted them to acknowledge Andrea's life. I didn't want to hear excuses. I wanted their contribution to mean more to them than it did . . . most of them had never met Andrea. Today part of me understands their reluctance to give, but it was never the monetary value, it was an acknowledgment of a cause in my life that has a very deep meaning. Today it still hurts. It just sticks with you."*

Wendy: *"Some relationships got stronger, the ones with the people who were there for me. I stopped speaking to some who weren't there."*

Common wisdom has it that people usually don't begin to face up to their own mortality until middle age. In our lives, we've had to deal with it far earlier. Sometimes we worry that what happened to them could happen to us.

Tom: *"You question your own mortality in a way. It's like watching yourself die. It was my first experience with death, and our lives had been so intertwined. It's the bigger picture of life and death you're dealing with. My brother died in a car accident. I don't think he was being reckless. We don't know what really happened. For quite a few years, he and I had both been daredevils and took risks."*

The brothers grew up in a car culture in which what you drove and how you drove it were an important part of who you were. Ironically, on the night he was killed, Michael was by himself and driving "the family tank," a heavy station wagon. Old habits are hard to shake and Tom continued to drive with abandon for a while after his brother's death. He was not consciously tempting fate, it was simply the way of life to which he was accustomed, but one which became less a part of him as he grew older.

Tom: *"I totaled a car the year after Michael died. I made sure I got home before the car was towed there. I knew they had to see me first. I drove crazy for a while, but I've calmed down now."*

Barry: *"It was my first experience with the death of anyone close to me. When you are young you don't really comprehend it. But I don't think when my sister died I thought of my own mortality."*

Allegra: *"I came to the realization that I am an only child and my parents are going to die someday and I'm going to be left alone. If I don't have some very good friends, I'm really in trouble."*

For our parents the deaths destroyed the joy of holidays and family occasions. We, too, were robbed of those times, although most of us now have the comfort of our own spouses and children.

Barry: *"The holidays are different for me now that I have my own kids. But they are still bittersweet. I don't want to say it's easier, but we try to spend as many holidays as we can together. Probably Mother's Day is the toughest and my sister's birthday and the anniversary of her death."*

Philip: *"As my other brother Eric and I have gotten older and started our families, I am aware that we are missing not only Howie, but the family he would have had. It creates some sadness that goes along with every celebration. It doesn't stop us from enjoying family gatherings, it's just something that is there."*

Holidays and special occasions mean greeting cards in our society, but it's very difficult for us to find cards that express love for our parents and yet acknowledge the loss that never leaves them.

Wendy: *"It's hard to find a card that doesn't show the perfect family. They all seem to say things such as, 'Mom, you are the best, you deserve the best,' but such words can be hurtful in our situation. I look and I analyze the cards. It's like walking on eggshells."*

Tom: *"I get blank cards."*

Debi: *"All those cards wishing you 'the best year ever.' It's not going to be the best year ever."*

Tom: *"Christmas used to be the four of us. Michael's absence becomes a huge presence."*

Allegra: *"Stuff that wouldn't even occur to me will set my parents off. Cards that wish the best year ever? Absolutely not. To me it's so benign, but everything takes on new connotations."*

Wendy: *"We changed our holidays. In the beginning my older sister had little kids and that was the only reason my mother continued doing anything. It was all for the grandchildren. We switched to having Chanukah at the club rather than at home."*

Now, when we look at our own children we can better understand the depth of our parents' loss. Having our own children has made us perhaps more wary than other parents. We have witnessed the fragility of life firsthand.

Abbe: *"I don't know that I am overly overprotective, but I have a lot of fears and anxieties about loss. When my kids were younger I went on field trips and drove places so as not to worry about transportation."*

Debi: *"Jess became an aunt to my children when she was seven years old.*

*Countless, joyful hours were spent with she and my children reading, playing games, baking cookies. They loved her with all their hearts and I loved that she was so much a part of their lives. A while after Jess died we renovated our home and my son had to take down the glow-in-the-dark stars that he and Jess had put up in his bedroom. He was extraordinarily upset since it was the last vestige of his contact with her. It broke my heart."*

Barry: *"You have a certain kind of love for your sibling. You are a family unit with deep feelings for one another, but when you have your own and feel the love for that child, you feel like 'wow,' you can't imagine the pain of losing a child. You see them grow up and they are a part of you, it's very different."*

Wendy: *"A sibling is devastating . . . but your own child. . . . I was one of three before Lisa died and I have two children. I told my gynecologist I wanted a third child and he asked why. When I told him he said that was the best reason he'd ever heard for having a third child."*

Barry: *"I told my daughter, 'I lost my sister in a car accident and I'm not losing you.' We are very strict about who she can get in a car with. Once she lied to us about who drove her home. I said, 'This is playing with fire and it's nonnegotiable.' Maybe you become more overprotective."*

Philip: *"I have learned from Howie's death how little in life we can control. I can be neurotic about safety on the school bus and it still may not matter. We couldn't protect Howie from everything and I can't protect my son from everything. That is the terrifying reality."*

Much like our parents, we questioned God. How could this happen? Could we still have any religious beliefs?

Tom: *"We were a religious family. Michael's death made me question God. Actually, I was always something of a doubter. Over the years I've walked away from organized religion . . . not because of my brother . . . but over the years. At first I felt there was no God, but I've found my way back."*

Nowadays, Tom's religion is more one of personal beliefs rather than part of any organized practice.

Tom: *"Over time, through an incredible amount of pain, I grew to understand things differently. I don't call it anything. No one has the answers. It's knowing there's a great power of energy out there. I don't need a man with a book telling me what to do. I realize there is no joy without suffering. No light without dark. I'm no longer daring death in a car or otherwise, because I'm no longer scared of it."*

Barry: *"I don't think it changed my religion one way or another. We looked to our rabbi for support, hoping he would have some answers. But, I don't think they enlighten you in any way as to why something like this happens. You just wonder who is responsible for letting this happen to your family."*

Philip: *"It has always bothered me that Judaism does not seem to acknowledge the sibling as a mourner. I attend the memorial service at Yom Kippur. In the prayer book there are prayers for those mourning a parent, a spouse, a child, but nothing for a sibling. We fall into the miscellaneous mourners category. It is jarring and hurtful. I have gone through periods of wanting to reject religion completely. On the other hand, I still identify with being a Jew."*

Wendy: *"My parents went to temple a lot in the year after. Something like going to temple to help the deceased's soul reach heaven. I kind of went for her and my family. But there are always questions . . . what did we do to deserve this?"*

Debi: *"Neither Judaism nor God had played any appreciable role in my life . . . but Jessica's death changed all that. On the day Jess died my daughter was to have her birthday party, but I could not get organized. I went out and bought a black dress that I did not even try on. When I returned home the telephone rang. It was my dad telling me Jess had been killed. A spiritual adviser later told me that an angel . . . possibly a deceased grandparent . . . had visited me on that day to help prepare me for the impending news of Jessica's death. Having had this spiritual connection, I now regularly pray to God and find enormous peace and comfort in my unwavering belief that my parents and I will again be with Jessica."*

Our mothers met through the Compassionate Friends support group. They took us to meetings, but none of us was able to bond with these groups.

Barry: *"I went to a meeting with my mother. I found it very difficult. There's a kind of guilt, like you're doing it for your parents, because it would make them feel good. I could see it really comforted these people at the meetings to see they are not alone, they're not crazy and these are normal feelings they are experiencing. But I was not keen on it."*

Wendy: "*My mother wanted me to go to a sibling support group, but I never went. I went to some meeting where the people were talking about losing someone who was like in their fifties. I couldn't understand what they were talking about. I walked out.*"

Debi: "*I went to one and heard parents saying their child had died ten years before and I thought, 'Oh, my God,' their grief is still fresh all these years later.*"

When Neill Perri died at the age of twenty-three, his brother Phillip was nineteen, and they were best friends. Asked to place something in Neill's casket, Phillip could only respond, "I'm placing my tears in with my brother." And so it is with most brothers and sisters who lose a sibling.

# Where We
# Are Now

For so long we have lived in our own small, sad cocoons, frozen in time, wrapped up in our own environment and oblivious to the outside world. Such an existence has provided us with a feeling of security, although we have learned the hard way that nothing in life is truly secure. Our detachment from our surroundings gave us the freedom to do only that which we could bring ourselves to focus upon, namely think about our lost children. The minutiae of everyday life dared not intrude upon our suffering.

Now our cocoons are opening, light is beginning to creep in where before there was only darkness. The physical and emotional pain that engulfed us for so long has begun to melt slowly away. In a strange way, we fear and even regret its passing. It has made for a constant bond with our dead children . . . and that was all we wanted.

At this point in our lives, we find we are becoming more absorbed in things we never thought we would care about again. This is a new road for us, one we take with trepidation because we have learned from personal tragedy that there is never any way to be certain of what lies ahead. We have no control over events. We did not choose this lot in life, but we do now choose to move forward. We believe strongly that this is the right road and the one our children would want us to walk.

We are nine mothers who carried our children within our bodies for nine months prior to their births and nurtured them into young adulthood. As we move ahead with our lives, we will continue to carry our children very much within ourselves until such time as we are with them again. . . . That is what mothers do.

# Author's Note

When I first agreed to collaborate on a book with nine bereaved mothers, I did so with mixed feelings. As a mother myself, I worried that their sorrow might overwhelm me.

And as I came to know the nine lost children intimately through their mothers, I would occasionally drive home in tears, reliving what could have been had these young people been given more time on earth.

My coauthors have opened their broken hearts, so that other bereaved parents might find comfort. Each of the nine is far stronger and has a greater capacity to love life than even they fully acknowledge or are perhaps too uncertain to admit even to themselves. I admire their indomitable courage.

I thank them for letting me share their innermost thoughts and emotions. They held nothing back and I am richer for having seen this too often incomprehensible world through their eyes.